Winning
the
Marriage
Marathon

Winning *the* Marriage Marathon

Six Strategies for Becoming Lifelong Partners

Gary P. Stewart
and
Timothy J. Demy

kregel
PUBLICATIONS

Grand Rapids, MI 49501

Winning the Marriage Marathon: Six Strategies for Becoming Lifelong Partners

Published by Kregel Publications, a division of Kregel, Inc., P.O. Box 2607, Grand Rapids, MI 49501. Kregel Publications provides trusted, biblical publications for Christian growth and service. Your comments and suggestions are valued.

The views represented in this volume are entirely those of the authors and do not reflect the position of any governmental agency or department.

Unless otherwise indicated, Scripture taken from the *Holy Bible: New International Version®.* © 1973, 1978, 1984 by International Bible Society. Used by permission of Zondervan Publishing House. All rights reserved.

Scripture quotations marked NASB are from the *New American Standard Bible,* © the Lockman Foundation 1960, 1962, 1963, 1968, 1971, 1972, 1973, 1975, 1977.

Scripture quotations marked NKJV are from the New King James Version.© 1979, 1980, 1982, Thomas Nelson, Inc., Publishers.

For more information about Kregel Publications, visit our web site: www.kregel.com

Cover and book design: Nicholas G. Richardson
Cover photo: PhotoDisc

Library of Congress Cataloging-in-Publication Data
Stewart, Gary P.
The marriage marathon: six strategies for becoming lifelong partners / Gary P. Stewart and Timothy J. Demy.
    p.   cm.
1. Married people—Religious life. 2. Marriage—Religious aspects—Christianity. I. Demy, Timothy J. II. Title.
BV4596.M3S75   1999   248.8'44—dc21   98-1529
                                CIP

ISBN 0-8254-2356-2

Printed in the United States of America
1 2 3 4 5 / 03 02 01 00 99

To Kathie Stewart and Lyn Demy
with great admiration and affection.
You have pursued the marriage marathon with us
and encouraged us throughout the journey.
Thank you, again and again.

Contents

⚞ Strategy 4 ⚟

Conflict Resolution: Seeking Growth in Times of Conflict   137

⚞ Strategy 5 ⚟

Goal-Setting: Planning Timely and Realistic Goals Together   159

⚞ Strategy 6 ⚟

Romance: Adding Zing to the Journey   175

Foreword

I've got to be honest. I've never run a marathon. For years I was the type of person who would get up in the morning and run around the block. Then I'd kick the block under the bed and go back to sleep! But a few years ago, I looked in the mirror and decided that something had to change—including my waist size! That's when I came up with the idea of running in a marathon. Unlike me at the time, most people I'd seen running in marathons looked to be in great shape. (Of course, I couldn't see the ones who were passed out in an oxygen tent!)

Possessing at least an 80 IQ (that means I usually can walk and chew gum at the same time), it dawned on me that it might take some training to run twenty-six miles. So I decided to run a "warm-up" race before entering the New York Marathon. Something a bit more manageable—say, a 10-K race in Green Lake, Wisconsin.

A 10-K race is the kind that gets you a neat T-shirt like in real marathons, but very few people end up on oxygen. That sounded good to me, so I signed up.

No training.

No preparation.

No special effort, other than buying new running shoes and a sharp new T-shirt. But, hey! How difficult could a measly 10-K race be, anyway?

I had no idea, as I lined up with a few hundred others, that "10-K" meant a six-mile-plus run. And in this case, it was six miles uphill the entire way! (Or at least it seemed that way.)

Don't get me wrong. I started well. I was right near the front of the pack. Surrounded by this thundering, running shoe-shod herd, I stayed with the leaders and fairly sprinted the first quarter mile. But then I hit the first hill . . . and then the second. I nearly fainted as I stopped (after what seemed like days) and drank every cup of water on a table with a sign attached that read "Halfway Point."

I wasn't ready for the race. I was *in* the race, and I wanted to finish well, but I'd spent more time picking out my wardrobe than training!

Many miles and minutes later, I finally staggered toward the finish line. There stood my faithful wife, Cindy, and my two precious daughters. When they saw me, they went crazy! They shouted and cheered. In fact, Kari and Laura both jogged with me across the finish line.

I was going to get my T-shirt after all!

You can't imagine how proud I felt when race personnel handed me the shirt. That's when my oldest daughter, Kari, put the race into perspective for me.

"Dad," she said, "we were worried about you!"

"Hey, I made it, didn't I?" I said, eyeing the oxygen tent as I staggered from the T-shirt table.

"Yeah, you made it. But when the lady with the jogging stroller came in so far ahead of you . . . well, we thought maybe you wouldn't."

What does being humiliated in a 10-K race by a mom with two kids in a stroller have to do with a book on marriage?

Actually, quite a bit.

When Cindy and I got married, I thought I was signing up for a sprint—lots of excitement and tons of adventure, romance, and encouragement. I didn't know what it took to run long distances with another person by my side. After all, I'd come from a single-parent home. I'd never seen, up close and personal, a couple who had stayed the course, much less won the race. I just knew I loved Cindy and wanted the T-shirt, so we got married.

But like that 10-K, there's more to a marriage than just starting well. We learned that the hard way, and so do many other people. These are people who, like Cindy and me, spend more time picking out a wedding dress and tux than learning what it takes to finish well.

I know now that a successful marriage isn't a dash—it's a marathon. It's hanging in there over the hills and through the miles. It's knowing when and how to take water breaks, and how to keep moving toward the finish line through each twist, turn, and trial.

That's why, if you're married or thinking seriously about getting married, you need to read this book. It's written by my good friends Gary Stewart and Tim Demy. They're marriage experts who can help prepare you for the realities of the road. They can make the training fun and the race far more enjoyable. They can work with you to help you be more in love tomorrow—miles farther down the road—than you are today. Like a cheering crowd, they'll encourage you up those tough hills and give you practical examples and take-immediately-to-the-track skills. And they'll show you how they've helped many couples cross the finish line together, still holding hands.

Your marriage may be at the start of the race, or perhaps you and your loved one are on your third or fourth decade together. There's biblical wisdom in this book for every couple. Gary and Tim combine solid scriptural insights with years of counseling experience and decades of service as military chaplains.

If you're serious about finishing the race and getting the T-shirt that says, "We finished well," you need a coach. Make it two coaches: Gary and Tim.

May the Lord bless you through every step, and every season, of your marriage.

JOHN TRENT, PH.D.
Author/Speaker
President, Encouraging Words

Acknowledgments

*T*his work is the result of several years of discussion, reading, and thought on the subject of marriage. Throughout this process, Jim Ellis has played an integral part in our marriage seminars. Thanks, Jim, for your thoughtful reflections, support, and the many great weekends we shared serving hundreds of couples. John Trent and Ken Gire have been mentors and friends, providing us with wisdom and kindness that can never be repaid. We encourage our readers to read their books and reflect on the contents of them.

We have been stimulated along the way by the encouragement, examples, and experiences of many couples who have confirmed to us the validity of the principles we present in the following pages. We especially want to thank Jim Ellis's wife, Shirley, Carl and Helga Henry, Jeff and Deb Ovall, Tommy and Janice Ice, Dave and Terri St. Pierre, and Ron and Sally Boss. Publisher Dennis Hillman has been a joy to work with and has enthusiastically guided us throughout the process. And, finally, from Gary to Lindsay, Jeff, and Katie: you are three of the four jewels upon the ring that surrounds my heart. Thanks to each of you.

Introduction

*M*any of us jump into things without much preparation. We figure that if we give something our best shot, one way or another it will work out. That approach often backfires. At some point, we have to bring everything to a stop, go back, reevaluate, and do the preparation we avoided in the first place.

Compare that approach with the planning done by cyclists who register for the famous *Tour de France* bicycle race or runners who enter the Boston Marathon. None of these participants would think they had a chance of winning these highly competitive endurance races without arduous preparation. They invest in the best equipment, train at high altitudes to improve their aerobic capacity, and gather the best sponsors and support teams they can find. Months and years of training are finally put to the test when the three-week race—lasting over twenty-four hundred miles—begins or the gun blast starts the twenty-six-mile foot race.

Whether we're participating in an athletic event, pursuing academic goals, or building successful relationships, preparation is key to success. In no situation is this more true than when building a marriage between two unique individuals. This effort takes physical, mental, emotional, and spiritual preparation. Some of us may have skipped the process of preparing for marriage. We may have plunged in without thought as to what was at stake. Now we may want to get our marriages back on course or be searching for ways to help us continue our successful journeys together as couples.

The good news is that we can take corrective action. Marriage is like an endurance cycling race on a tandem bicycle. We can make course corrections, learn ways to pull together as a team, and enjoy the journey itself. By the way, our goal in this marriage marathon is not to come in first. Like the participants in a race who are simply trying to achieve their best time ever, we want to complete the course and finish well. To reach this goal, all have to register, prepare, come together at the starting line, and live the journey to the finish line. We aren't competing against other couples. For this reason, we will usually refer to the marathon as a *journey rather than a race*.

The key to completing the marriage marathon is found in preparation and application. Will we consistently apply the principles we learn to our journey together? Will we try to ride as if we are on separate bikes, or will we realize that as a couple we are actually on a tandem bicycle and need to work together? Simply finishing does not prove that our journey was successful. *How we ride the course* ultimately determines our success. Two components lead to a successful journey: motivation and personal commitment.

Motivation

Gary first met Carla in a hospital room. She was curled up in the corner on a stool, wearing a pink sweat suit and looking like she had just lost the most important race of her young life. Certain that the future looked as dim as her dark past, she had attempted to end her life earlier that day. Carla had been married about five years, was the mother of three children, and had a husband who genuinely loved her. This twenty-six-year-old woman appeared aged by the experiences of a past that would not relinquish her. She was tired of living and was certain that she had nothing to offer her family and community. She was convinced that her past had locked her into a future that could only bring pain and emptiness to everything she touched and anyone she knew. What she perceived as her "unchangeable past" made suicide her unavoidable future. Her life was nearly cut short because she believed that how she viewed the horrible experiences of her childhood could not be changed.

Healing the Wounded Heart

Carla's experiences will always be part of her past, but they do not have to determine her future or continue to carry the same influence. Their weight can be regularly diminished by her focus on the good that she creates and experiences in her present. How we live today determines what our past will be tomorrow.

Few of us would deny that our past has much to do with our present—with who we are today. Previous experiences, good and bad, affect how we live in the present and potentially how we live in the future. The principles we learn from our parents, whether good or bad, become the principles of today, unless something else in our past (such as a spiritual conversion) redirects us. Proverbs teaches us that if we remember the teaching we received from godly parents, we will avoid committing abominations that God hates (Prov. 6:16–20). Counselors are convinced that past experiences shape our present attitudes. Without changed beliefs and a thorough understanding of our faulty thinking, our future will be a carbon copy of our past. People need to *create a new past* by making good decisions in the present. Remember, tomorrow your today will be in the past. In this somewhat awkward statement lies the starting point from which Carla began to believe that she could be a positive participant in her marriage.

We need to *live today in such a way that tomorrow we can look back to a better past*. The more constructive or positive days we experience, the more yesterdays we have to remind us of what tomorrow has the potential to be. We can change the negative influence of the past by learning to live by principles that protect us from personal and relational harm. In time, the past that confused and misled us will be less influential than the more recent past that has brought us peace and growth. A past built on proven principles motivates us to live faithfully today.

Many of us brought a lot of baggage into our marriages. We might not be able to get rid of the old baggage, but developing new baggage (healthy experiences) can help us leave our old baggage gathering dust in the attic of our minds. Like Carla, many of us lived through difficult experiences before we got married. These experiences have the potential to cause any number of difficulties. Though our past experiences will never be forgotten, they can play less of a role as we apply the principles of marriage that are provided throughout this book. These principles will help us endure the normal obstacles of the journey and enjoy the confidence that comes from being well prepared to go the distance. As we care for and respect our spouses day after day, discuss difficult issues without being defensive, forgive, plan and execute goals, and encourage continued courtship, we create a past that becomes the impetus for hope tomorrow. Victories today build confidence to face tomorrow. Your marriage matters; work on it so that it will be stronger tomorrow than it was yesterday or is today!

It Takes Heart

You would think that the purchase of a marriage book or attendance at a marriage seminar would indicate that we care about our marriages, but appearances are sometimes deceiving. Some of us go to a seminar because we want to stay married but can't seem to make it work. Some of us go because our spouses made us or because we know our spouses would like it. Still others of us may think learning marriage principles or attending a seminar has the magical "something" that will turn things around. But learning principles for succeeding in the marriage marathon is not enough. Whether we carry the old baggage of a difficult past, as Carla did, or we had a great childhood, the attitude we bring to our marriages is a primary indicator of how successful our marriages will be. *Attitude* has a lot to do with whether we end up exhausted and quit the marathon or find ourselves exhilarated and endure. You must *care about your marriage* enough to work hard at making it a positive growing experience. Without an attitude of concern for others, marriage becomes an experiment rather than a journey.

Caring is what makes our belief in and application of principles effective. We must nurture an attitude that says, I will learn and apply information that helps me help those I care about. Caring eliminates the facades that people wear as they attempt to fool others or meet society's expectations. Caring is a sign that there is a touch of love governing our decisions. Caring makes commitment a lifelong endeavor. Ross Campbell expressed the importance of a caring attitude when he wrote:

> If we continue to carry out our marital responsibility as a lifelong commitment, we will grow together in love, appreciation, and respect. *We must live and think as if there are no other alternatives than to make this marriage work.* Yes, it is work. It is hard work. And it takes this lifelong commitment of both spouses.[1] (emphasis added)

We can say that we care, but our attitudes are always betrayed by our actions. We toy with reality because we hate stigmas or anything that might suggest failure. How many times have we heard divorced people say that they are good friends who simply could not live together? Actor Kevin Costner admitted, "I try to conduct my life with a certain amount of dignity and discretion—but marriage is a hard, hard gig."[2] He believed that the difficulties of marriage were too hard for him to overcome. But as we listen to many divorced people, we must wonder if they really cared about the welfare of their families *more* than their own welfare. Often the honest answer is no. Until we link the principles of marriage and commitment with an attitude of caring, we will continue to deceive ourselves about our sinful tendencies or keep them concealed in the closet of human weakness and depravity. It may be hard to say that we don't care, but until we learn to admit the truth, we will continue to dissolve marriages and damage family members. *I care means I stay and make the necessary changes to make my staying beneficial to the family.* Do we really care?

The Hebrew word *leb* and the Greek word *kardia* are translated "heart" in the Bible. Both terms are used literally and metaphorically. The metaphorical use of the words will help us understand the attitude that is required if our marriage marathons are going to be successfully completed.

The heart is the center of everything that comprises personhood. Hans Walter Wolff wrote that the heart is "the most important term in the vocabulary of Old Testament anthropology."[3] It describes our courage (2 Chron. 17:6) and our lack thereof (Deut. 20:3), positive emotion (Deut. 19:6; 28:47; John 16:22; Acts 2:26; Eph. 6:22) and anguish (Deut. 15:10; Jer. 4:19; John 16:6; Rom. 9:2). The heart is connected with knowledge and understanding. It is the source of thought and reflection (1 Kings 3:12; Prov. 19:8; John 12:40; Heb. 4:12), but this knowledge can be deceitfully wicked as well (Prov. 10:20–21; Jer. 17:9; Matt. 15:19; Rom. 2:5; Heb. 3:12). The heart is also the catalyst for volition or intention, whether referring to God (1 Sam. 2:35; Jer. 23:20) or to people (Ezra 7:10; 1 Kings 8:17; Dan. 1:8; 2 Cor. 9:7). It includes evil intentions as well (Rom. 1:24; Acts 8:22). The word is also used to describe emotions, intellect, and will. Within the heart lies everything that is both good and bad about humankind. It is the place where God looks to judge the value of a person's service or worship (Mark 7:6) and the place where genuine conversion to God takes place (Ps. 51:10).[4] In his excellent work *In Search of the Heart,* Dr. David Allen describes the heart as

> the place that is most personal but also most universal since we reach out to others through our hearts. It is the dwelling

place of our values, our love, our commitment, our dreams. It is the source of our attitudes, intentions, and behaviors. It is the repository of good and evil, love and hate—the place where we touch the divine.[5]

The heart is the aspect of our humanity that each day we must confront and challenge with biblical principles because it is not only "the place where we touch the divine," it is also the place where the divine touches us. It is at the core of our hearts that we must choose to let truth make its mark on the marriage marathon. The marital blueprint that God provides in His Word can touch and change the heart of the individual in ways not fully known to us. The depth of the heart's depravity is unknown (Jer. 17:9). Therefore only God and His truth can create lasting change (1 Cor. 4:5; Rom. 8:27; 1 Thess. 2:4).

It is our hope that the introduction of biblical truth into the heart of each reader will induce healing, change, and growth. For our attitude to be at its best, we must open our hearts to the Surgeon who can correct the attitude of the heart from one of selfish ambition to one of selfless association. The successful marriage marathon takes two people working together for each other's benefit. Hopefully the change that you experience intellectually as you read this book will be used by the Holy Spirit to soften and open your heart toward emotional, volitional, and spiritual renewal. It is in the corrupt heart, the center of all we are, that God initiates His work of redemption (Rom. 8:27; 10:6–10). Therefore, it is to the hearts of couples contaminated by the cancer of sin, hurt by careless hands, wounded by unfulfilled wishes, and aching for meaningful and growing associations with their spouses, friends, and family that this book is directed.

Ideally, marriage is a place where the heart finds refuge from the daily struggles of human existence. It should be a place of celebration where two hearts rejoice in the development of an unconditional love that they alone nurture to share with the world. It is a place of beginning, a place of commitment, a place where the candle of hope is never extinguished. Ultimately, marriage is a precursor of the relationship the church will one day have with its groom, the Lord Jesus Christ. *Without God's direction, winning the marriage marathon is a possibility; with God's direction, it is a certainty* that is daily pursued with a hope that ensures mutual companionship all the way to the finish line. We must live marriage according to the guidelines of its Designer or suffer damage from architectural weakness. A marriage that ignores biblical principles may be able to stand, but it is certain to lack structural integrity.

Personal Commitment

What is the underlying ingredient that makes a relationship possible? Some would argue that love is the basic ingredient to success in marriage, but the love with which humans enter relationships in most cases is extremely immature. Our human nature lacks the understanding and depth of love required to sustain a lasting relationship. Something is needed to qualify (assess how good or genuine) and quantify (measure how much) an individual's "true" love.

Consider the response of a person who, when asked, "Would you like to ride in a bicycle marathon?" answers, "Oh yes, *I love* to ride, so I'm confident the experience would be quite rewarding!" Do you think that the individual's love for riding bikes is enough to ensure a rewarding experience? If the person loves to ride bikes but has little desire to finish the course, a rewarding experience might be possible; but most people who start a race want to finish it. Loving to ride will not guarantee that they make it to the finish line. Regardless of how much we love something, young or immature love is not sufficient to guarantee success. I may love to eat apple pies, but if I am unwilling to go to the store or to an orchard to pick my own apples, I will never enjoy the taste of a fresh apple pie.

The same is true with relationships. We may believe we have a deep and lasting love for our spouses, when in fact, our love has not been challenged sufficiently to ensure that it will endure the changes and difficulties that confront most, if not all couples. So what is it that qualifies and quantifies the love that we as spouses offer? How do we know if that love is lacking? The quality of our love is defined by the *commitments* that we make and keep.[6] Blind love steps out to pursue and initiate a relationship; the level or genuineness of commitment determines whether that love will grow sufficiently to sustain a meaningful and lasting relationship.

A friend of Gary's recently began to put his love of running to the test. Though he loved to run, was he willing to advance in the running world to another level, a level that would bring greater satisfaction? How much did he really love running? *Did he love it enough to work through the challenges to reap its greatest benefits?* To find out, he had to establish certain commitments, which he had to adhere to, to ensure his love for running would not be limited by the challenges that accompany the distance one must cover to complete a marathon. His commitments have helped him to improve his performance over the past year and continue running. An unchallenged love for running got him into the sport; a challenged love, kept alive and growing through his personal commitments, guaranteed completion of the course.

Marriage works the same way. Numerous couples have answered the question, "Why do you want to marry?" with the standard response, "Because we are in love!" They naively think that they understand the depth (quality and quantity) of their love without it ever being tested. They confidently exclaim, "Love will be enough!" For them, commitment is a natural corollary of love, an obvious extension of the feelings that permeate all their senses, rather than a mutually selected list of mandates or statements that define their love and the direction they desire their marriages to take.

Reality shows that personal commitments are not the natural corollary of a love that is corrupted by human nature saturated with the sinful consequences of the Fall (Gen. 3; Rom. 3:9–20). Rather, commitments are the demanding choices we make to identify and contain the selfish tendencies of our hearts so that our innate desire to love can be shaped and matured by learned biblical principles. Personal commitment is the hinge on which love swings from closed (selfish) to open (selfless). It is essential for any couple hoping to complete the marriage marathon.

When Marc and Christine were married, they sincerely believed that they loved one another enough to face the challenges of the most difficult marathon. As time passed, the vows they had shared on their wedding day became distant memories. Christine was disillusioned by a husband who was driven to occupational excellence in order to ensure that their three children were cared for and retirement would arrive before age fifty-five. Marc was frustrated by a wife who loved buying things for the children and their home rather than building a nest egg for a retirement that seemed ages away.

Many couples, faced with similar experiences, express their new realization with the infamous words, "I don't think we love each other anymore." It is more accurate to say that these couples either didn't love each other at the outset or that the love they had early in their marriage was insufficient to handle the challenges of married life. The latter is more often the truth. We all begin marriage with what we might call an innate love or desire to love that is more feeling than substance. This innate love draws us together, but it is wholly insufficient for going the distance. So it needs to be honed by mutually-agreed-upon commitments.

Herein lies the uniqueness of this book. *The topics we will discuss do not cover a selected set of marriage principles that seem to be disconnected from each other. Rather, these principles are linked together by personal commitments that consistently and regularly challenge the quality of our love.* Marc and Christine never recognized the shortcomings of innate love. Because they equated love with commitment or had not agreed upon a mutual set of commitments to shape their love, their immature love was denied the opportunity to mature into a love that ignores feelings and overcomes the inevitable failings on the part of both spouses to ensure unity.

For love to mature, commitments must be established. Each topic discussed in this book introduces a *strategy* statement that calls for a personal commitment to a biblical principle. Successful marathons demand serious strategies. As you progress through the book, notice that each strategy statement is connected to the previous one in the same way that the rungs of a ladder are attached to the rails. All statements build on the principles that precede them. The sequential nature of the strategy statements unites the sessions into a single plan, leading to a successful completion of the marriage marathon.

It is difficult to snuggle on the couch (romance, part 6) when we are unsure of the course we are running (goal-setting, part 5) because of an unresolved conflict (conflict resolution, part 4) that was created by inadequate communication skills (communication, part 3). We don't communicate well with a person for whom we have little respect (key ingredients, part 2), and we cannot easily love or respect a person about whom we know very little (spouse-centered living, part 1). This book is designed to help spouses see marriage as a process of interlinking principles that work together for the benefit of their marriages. Many books address the topics discussed in this book individually, but few, if any, make the necessary connections between them.

The strategy begins with part 1, "Spouse-Centered Living: Putting First Things First," and ends with part 6, "Romance: Adding Zing to the Journey." The following strategy statements provide verbal commitments that, if practiced daily, will gradually deepen the innate love that initially attracted you to your spouse. They are:

I will place my spouse's needs before my own.

I will daily love, honor, and encourage my spouse.

I will practice a style of communication that allows my spouse to be vulnerable and honest at all times.

I will seek resolution and growth during conflict.

I will set timely and realistic goals with my spouse.

I will nurture romance through daily care.

Let's begin. You *can win* the marriage marathon!

🌿 Strategy One 🌿

I will place my spouse's
needs before my own.

Spouse-Centered Living: Putting First Things First

Why do so many couples begin the marriage marathon but fail to finish it? Perhaps it is because we've bought into the philosophy that marriage is for me, and it is my spouse's responsibility to meet my needs. This perspective is not accurate; if left unchallenged and unchanged, it will lead to frustration and failure. It is only when we attempt to meet the needs of our spouses 100 percent of the time that we give marriage the opportunity to progress and succeed. This is an idealistic goal and is difficult to maintain consistently; nevertheless, commitment to this goal pushes each marriage partner away from the selfish tendency to create relationships for personal or individual gain and forms an essential part of the groundwork upon which a healthy relationship depends.

Men and women are different physically, emotionally, sexually, and spiritually. Acceptance and knowledge of these differences provide us with information to better understand the needs and idiosyncrasies of our spouses. If we ignore the differences, we ignore the needs. When we ignore the needs, we ignore the spouses, leaving them open to isolation and loneliness. Marriage is a marathon that can be won, but it requires that the couple ride tandem if they expect to cross the finish line together. It is important that we mutually apply and responsibly commit to the first strategy statement: *"I will place my spouse's needs before my own."*

Marriage Strategy I

Without a growing knowledge of the person you marry, love becomes stale. With misunderstanding, love becomes frustrated. When there is no understanding, love moves on. Knowledge of the one you desire to love gives you an understanding of his or her history and unique needs. If you don't learn about your spouse's past, including fears, joys, and in general the ways in which your spouse is different from you, your love for your spouse will not mature and you will be unable to meet his or her needs. And if you fail to meet needs, you send a message to your spouse that he or she is less important than you. This failure turns the marriage marathon into a slow and tedious uphill ride that leads to exhaustion and eventually to quitting the race.

Every race needs a strategy for dealing with problems that may arise as the journey progresses. You must commit yourself to becoming sensitive to your spouse's needs by seeking to understand your unique differences as male and female. Without this understanding, it's difficult—if not impossible—to meet needs. Once you understand the "baggage" of your spouse's past and the differences that exist between you, you can then *choose to commit yourself* to meeting the needs that these differences create.

The choice or strategy to "place my spouse's needs before my own" flies straight in the face of the "me first" philosophy. The idea that we are to take care of our own needs first so that we will then have the strength to focus on the needs of others undermines our desire to build our relationships with our spouses on the foundation of love. Our personal needs are sometimes too complex and varied to assume that we can meet them independently of others, and our human nature is too suspect to suggest that each of us can know when our personal needs are met adequately enough to begin helping another. It is unthinkable that riders on a tandem bicycle would be thinking of their own needs and desires separately from those of the partner on whom they depend for safety and success. Both riders must be continually aware of the needs of the other!

CHAPTER 1

Failing to Reach the Finish Line

$\mathscr{L}$ ife at warp speed" is a phrase that many of us can probably use to describe the challenges and chaos in our daily lives. In our fast-paced, high-tech, mobile society, we search for stability and strength in many places, especially in our relationships, communities, and careers. The one place where we should always find satisfaction is in the safe confines of a loving relationship with our spouses—persons to whom we are fully devoted and who are fully developed to us in return. Unfortunately, this is not always the case, nor is it the standard for our times. All too often, the hope for stability ends in the heartache of isolation and loneliness. As noted earlier, marriage is, as one popular personality stated, "a hard, hard gig."[1]

You Don't Bring Me Flowers Anymore

Too many individuals make the mistake of assuming that their own significance and stability lie in the commitment of their spouses toward them, when in reality, the strength of a relationship comes from what *one spouse gives, sacrifices, and devotes to or for the other*. Instead of being concerned with what we can give to our spouses, we too often focus on what we think our spouses should be giving us. We drain our spouses of strength without realizing or remembering that we must also be a source of strength for the persons we promised to love. This failure to give has resulted in the deterioration and disillusionment of many contemporary marriages. Relationships that began with the endearing words "I do" end with the bang of a judge's gavel and the words "divorce granted."

Unanswered Questions

Why do so many marriages fail? Where has the stability gone? Why have so many dreams been needlessly shattered? What has driven us to place so much pressure on our spouses to satisfy *our* needs? What has captivated so much of our time that we have placed the concerns of others below our own? How is it that a marriage can turn from ecstasy to agony and from bliss to blitz in less time than it takes for ink to dry on a marriage license? We marry for happiness, devotion, peace, security, and romance only to find fulfillment of these desires elusive or nonexistent. Our hopes and desires wither and die like rose petals falling to the ground.

As we enter marriage, we often find ourselves stepping into a wilderness of human differences; our vows turn to vapor and our dreams to dismay. Marriage is, as proclaimed in a recent *Time* magazine cover-story, "an activity that everyone—save perhaps the most wildly romantic and misguided among us—has come to regard as a sometimes thrilling sometimes infuriating, but always necessary exercise."[2]

Storm-Gale Relationships

Because of the struggles people have seen in their own marriages and in those of others, the institution of marriage has become suspect. It has been pulled from its moorings, leaving many couples adrift in a sea of despondency or crushed on the rocks of divorce. No longer is marriage seen as a place of refuge, a safe haven. Rather, it is often seen as something temporary, expendable, uncertain, and therefore unnecessary. This perspective has all too often brought death rather than health to many marriages.

Race to the Finish

It takes two to make a marriage but only one to tear it apart. Each partner requires support if success is to be expected; a spouse whose needs are left unmet can only persevere so long before becoming exhausted. In a bicycle marathon, no one wins alone or without support, especially if they are riding tandem. Success depends on both riders. Marriage demands the same: two people devoted to learning the needs of each other and being committed to meeting them. Only then can the course be completed successfully. We can build our relationships into teams that are capable of completing the marriage marathon. Go for the finish line, and those who stand on the sidelines and watch will see a great display of God's unconditional love and devotion in you, your spouse, and your marriage!

Anyone who has watched or participated in any kind of race has witnessed many who have crossed the finish line successfully and others who, for a variety of reasons, failed to reach it. Our emotions are instinctively drawn to both types of racers, but the emotions we feel are quite different. For the victors we cheer, and for those who fail we sigh and cry, knowing that their mistakes will be endlessly replayed and analyzed in their minds.

According to the Scriptures, God intends that a husband and wife remain together as "one flesh" for as long as both live, that is, until death separates them (Gen. 2:21–25; Mal. 2:13–16; Matt. 5:32; Mark 10:5–9; 1 Cor. 7:1–11). Competing in and finishing the marriage marathon is, therefore, an act of faithfulness (obedience and trust) to God and a calling that protects and nourishes each partner and the children they produce (Mal. 2:15; 1 Cor. 7:14; Eph. 5:22–33). A successful marriage also reflects the oneness and character of God. It is God's desire that marriage be a divine illustration of unconditional, perpetual love. True love is an unconditional commitment to an imperfect person for life. (Isn't that how God loves us?) Unfortunately that is not everyone's understanding or experience in marriage. Imperfect people in an imperfect world often falter in the marathon of marriage. Some get up and start again at the beginning; some get up and keep going from where they failed; others, too bruised, broken, or exhausted, don't get up at all, or if they do, they just walk away. But why do they falter in the first place? Why do they take a wrong turn, trip on the obstacles, or not pace themselves properly? Did they not understand the course, or did they simply underestimate its challenges? Whatever the reasons, too many couples don't complete the journey.

Who's in the Mirror?

Reflect for a few minutes on your marriage. As you peer into that relational mirror, who and what do you see? Are you enamored with her beauty or his physique? Was his confidence a balance to your shyness? Did her gentle spirit balance your candidness? Did you see in him an opportunity for happiness and success, or in her a complementary personality that enhanced the image you desire? Was he hope for you, or was she your strength? He the perfect father, she the child's delight? Is the marriage you see before you an image of mutual or individual happiness? Do you smile alone, or does your spouse join you? Is one spouse in the foreground and the other hidden in the shadows; are you side by side or do you look in the mirror and realize that you have been so focused on yourself that your spouse is not even visible? Too often, we lose sight of our spouses. By failing to recognize the presence and importance of our spouses to the relationship, we deceive ourselves and destroy the ones we thought we loved. The mirror is shattered, and the marathon is lost.

Me First!

The prevailing philosophy of our culture that distorts our image of marriage is one that proclaims sometimes clearly, but *often covertly,* that "Marriage is for me. My spouse will be there to meet my needs and expectations." We think: "I'll do my part, my spouse will do his or her part, and all will be great. My spouse will be the perfect person to fill the holes in my life and help me be what I've wanted to be. We're good for each other, and I've got a great catch. I know it'll be all right, I've got it all planned. What could go wrong when it feels so right? Every day's a picnic or Saturday night!"

In this somewhat exaggerated scenario, the issues, thoughts, feelings, wants, and desires of our spouses are mistakenly assumed to be the same as our own. Ultimately the "me first" spouse will look to the side, only to discover that his or her spouse is no longer along for the ride or has been left far behind.

So What?

What are the consequences if we consciously or unconsciously embrace a philosophy in which we focus on our own needs before those of our spouses? The consequences are many, and they are harmful. If we expect harmony and growth, we will be greatly surprised, for the fruit that is borne from selfishness is surely bitter and never sweet. Here are nine such bitter fruits that result from deciding to ignore the needs of our spouses.

1. Siphoned Significance

When we forget or ignore the theological fact that our creation in the image of God gives personal significance and dignity to every individual, we exchange the truth for a lie. Our estimation of our personal worth becomes skewed. This misjudgment and deception is tragic, for it affects all those with whom we come in contact, especially our spouses. We attempt to siphon from our spouses the significance we crave, rather than recognizing and accepting the inherent significance the two of us share as creations of God who are fearfully and wonderfully made. Our personal happiness and contentment become dependent upon another person's treatment of us. Sometimes knowingly, but often unknowingly—like a haze from the sea that gradually engulfs us—we make ourselves superior to our spouses and use them to provide that which God has already given us. As creatures of God, we are inherently significant. As we nurture our relationship with Him, there is little need to siphon significance from others.

It is impossible for an imperfect person to carry the burden of continuously giving affirmation or appreciation to another without receiving it in return. When we selfishly demand care and attention from our spouses to validate our own existence and ideas, we eventually dismiss criticism and reject our spouses' input or participation in the relationship. The problem with selfishness is that it takes from another and gives nothing in return.

Sometimes we marry naively, thinking that our spouses will always validate our emotions, tolerate our idiosyncrasies, and share the same dreams. As a result, any variation or rejection causes us to protect ourselves from the threat of perceived injury, rather than accepting constructive criticism as a potential for growth. The spouses we depend upon to help us fulfill our desires are forced into an either/or situation in which they cannot win. *Either* our partners accept our plans, ultimately being drained of individuality and involvement in the relationship, *or* our spouses continue to express their concerns and ideas until we accuse them of failing to meet our needs. This situation causes us to drain our spouses of their personalities, creativity, and dreams. Over time, this siphoning leaves our spouses uninvolved in the daily development of the marriage and ultimately demeaned. We enjoy the passing moments of a tenuous marriage, ignoring the fact that eventually our spouses will be drained of self-respect and dignity and have nothing left to give. Such a marriage will end in tragedy, even if the couple doesn't get divorced. The hope of a common journey ends on separate paths of despair and disappointment.

2. Limited Love

Another consequence of focusing on our own needs is limited love (selfish love), which says in effect, "I won't give what I don't get." Such an attitude makes love for our partners conditional—willingness to give love is based upon first receiving love. We find ourselves trapped in the reality of our own humanity, unable to escape the spiritual bondage that confines us to our own self-interest.

For the Christian, conditional or limited love is a paradox. Because God has indeed "first loved us," a spouse's love should never be the impetus for giving love. We love our spouses as a reflection and response of God's love for us. "I love my spouse because God loved me" (cf. John 13:34). Until the love of God transforms the human heart, limited love is our only recourse. It remains limited until a genuine understanding of what God's love has accomplished in and for us breaks through our shell of selfishness. To break through this shell, we need to remind ourselves daily of the sacrifice of Jesus Christ in both His life and death. It is through an understanding and personal application of this selfless act that the true potential of love is awakened, a love that sacrifices itself for the benefit of another.

Without this daily reminder, our love remains no more than a morning dew that covers the grass until the heat of the day burns it away. Our daily activities become routine exercises that preoccupy our minds, while concern for others is pushed to the side. The person who subscribes to the "me first" philosophy either ignores or is oblivious to the effect of the day's heat on others, focusing on his or her own comfort and needs. Limited love leaves a once hopeful spouse longing to be heard and a needy child craving for acceptance in an environment he or she can't understand or alter.

But the effects of limited love don't stop here. Limited love forces its adherents on a journey that leads to emotional turmoil and loneliness as they push aside those who long to be their companions. Truly, the reward of *me first* is *me only*. Unable to share the warmth and security of genuine love, we are left with burned-out relationships and scorched hearts. Limited love is really no love at all because it is undependable and subjective, serving the server more than the recipient. It only provides a pittance of what boundless and unconditional love can actually give.

3. Abandoned Affection

If we continue to focus on our own needs rather than those of our companions, we will not only siphon our significance from them and limit the nature and amount of love we provide to them, but we will inevitably cause them to feel unappreciated and unwanted. By continually giving without receiving anything in return, our spouses become physically and emotionally weary and believe that we have abandoned our affection for them.

The psychological need to be known and loved by others is an enormous desire. Affection gives a person a sense of belonging and purpose. Affection is one of the reasons we marry. People need to feel cared for, have someone who worries about their welfare and personal growth, and know that there is at least one person who favors them above everyone else. The absence of affection causes us to doubt our self-worth. We all want to have someone who is concerned about us when we drive along a lonely road late at night, are caught out in a storm, or are facing a difficult day or challenge. We want someone with whom we can share our fears and failures, our tears and triumphs, and our dreams and desires. Someone who will smile but not laugh, teach but not taunt, hold but not handle, empower rather than exhaust. Prolonged loss of affection leads us to self-preservation. Without intervention, the unloved person becomes unloving.

Even when we experience personal struggles and feel drained, affection or concern for the welfare of others should not be diminished. Affection does not exist in a vacuum. It is the product of having experienced love from others. Only as we give affection to our spouses will we be able to receive a continual flow of affection in return. We can tell we have abandoned affection toward our partners when we hear statements such as, "I'm tired of giving and not getting anything in return," or "I gave and gave and gave and now there's nothing left to give," or "I feel so empty, I have nothing left to share." Reciprocal care and concern is necessary if a marriage expects to grow and thrive. Daily affection is not an option; it is the pulse of a healthy marriage. Without it, there is no love. Its absence exposes the absence of love.

4. Excluded Existence

Ultimately, if we have a "me first" philosophy in our marriages, we will find ourselves living an excluded existence. "We are living two separate lives under one roof" becomes the spoken or unspoken reality of a relationship that is a thin facade of its original form. The biblical maxim that "a household divided against itself will not stand" becomes a painful and repeated ordeal in too many lives. Eventually we will focus on ourselves—independent of our spouses—for protection and preservation. Our partners will do the same. When this happens, an intimate relationship erodes into an excluded existence. Hopes and dreams of happiness and togetherness are washed away by tears of frustration, loneliness, and isolation.

Marriage demands a commitment to unity that finds cohesion through mutual devotion. The union must be greater than its individual parts. Its potential is dependent upon the ability and willingness of each partner to focus on the individual potential of the other. It is only as we grow both individually and as a couple that satisfaction and security become reality. Anything short of total commitment opens the door to loneliness and a resurgence of the "me first" approach to marriage. We start our marriages longing for the companionship it offers but fail to recognize the selfish motives that prevent us from reaching that goal. Excluded existence is the result. Tandem bikes are built for two; it is never intended that they be ridden by a single rider. The same is true of marriage.

5. Impaired Intimacy

Intimacy is the product of daily care and affection. The closeness we feel toward our spouses is directly dependent upon the care we maintain over an extended period of time. Anytime there is friction between spouses, the depletion of intimacy is one of the first stress fractures to appear. If left unnoticed and unresolved, that fracture will continue to expand until it leads to a clean break. Trying to maintain a marriage without intimacy is like trying to win a marathon with a broken leg. It may be possible, but the going is slow, painful, and thoroughly undesirable. Feelings of rejection, woundedness, worthlessness, and hopelessness may keep us from even wanting to be in the same room with our spouses. Lack of care slowly drives a wedge between a couple, putting pressure on their commitment until the relationship shatters. As long as the wedge exists, intimacy is as elusive as water in the desert. The marriage becomes nothing more than a mirage, and the marathon is in jeopardy of ending or, at best, slows to a crawl.

Intimacy or closeness results from constantly acting toward our spouses in ways that raise his or her self-esteem and sense of being valued. It comes from attentive listening, encouraging, approving, sharing, and comforting. Ultimately it brings greater pleasure to the relationship, strengthens our confidence, and creates an atmosphere that allows the sexual aspect of marriage to be a pleasure rather than merely a duty or painful necessity.

Several signs that marriage is losing its closeness are diminished communication, lack of affection, infrequent interaction, and decreased touching. As these elements diminish, conflict, agitation, and isolation increase. The loss of intimacy is painful. It is an emptiness that reaches deep into our souls and yearns for satisfaction. This loss will inevitably occur when one or both spouses adopt a "me first" mentality.

6. Conditional Commitment

Selfishness can only produce limited devotion. Commitments of a "me first" spouse are only as strong as the commitments the other spouse is willing to make. Rather than striving to understand the commitments of others, the selfish spouse tends to express affection only for personal gain. "If I get, then I can give." The relationship is manipulative at its core, and bitter for both.

The development of trust is jeopardized when the loyalty or devotion of one spouse is questioned. "I just don't know how we are going to make it if you don't see the importance of what I'm saying." "If you're not going to be there for me; what am I to think?" Statements that associate disagreement or hesitancy with disloyalty become commonplace in a relationship with conditional commitment. Regardless of which spouse is speaking, both will lose. Conditional commitments are found in any sentence that forces one spouse to accept the other's agenda. This situation sacrifices mutual understanding and equates loyalty with blind submission or trust. One spouse becomes a puppet on a string manipulated by the actions of the other. In such relationships, trust cannot be nurtured, so suspicion becomes a daily habit.

In a healthy relationship, commitment is not given on the basis of good or bad decisions, emotional satisfaction, or mutual agreement and support. Commitment is not an option or something for which we barter. Rather, commitment is an indicator and an expression of true love. Commitment transcends the fluctuation of emotions, the uncertainty that comes with change, and the aging that comes with the passing of time. It ensures that the security of our marriage is never in question. Failure, illness, disappointment, and loss must never jeopardize any commitment that supports a marriage. Lasting relationships are dependent upon commitments that compliment forgiveness and trust. When trust is limited, suspicion fills the void.

The consequence of limited trust is unlimited suspicion. Commitments create an environment for trust to grow, keeping the "me first" tendency in check and the marriage marathon on course.

7. Rejected Responsibility

"You're the reason this marriage isn't working." "If you would change, I would work harder at this relationship." Comments such as these reflect the selfish and nonsacrificial attitude of a spouse who rejects responsibility for the relationship. Blame is cast on the partner for all marriage problems. Unwillingness to face the mutual responsibilities of committed love leads to emotional finger-pointing, and the marriage begins to unravel.

Blame places the effort for making a successful marriage squarely on the shoulders of one spouse. If we have a condemning attitude, we perceive our marriage problems as resulting from anything or anyone other than ourselves. Placing blame, whether justified or not, puts a spouse in a defensive posture. This lessens the possibility for open exchange or interaction. Even when blaming seems appropriate, it is better to work toward some kind of resolution to the conflict in a composed, selfless manner. The goal is to find common ground for growth, not to accentuate the differences that divide.

When we accept responsibility in our marriages, we create a safe environment for failure. The freedom to fail without criticism enables us to change and grow without fear. Partners in the marriage marathon share the responsibility to heal a spouse's wounded heart rather than haunt it. A predator attacks, but a partner guards and protects. Abandoning responsibility will hasten the death of a marriage. Where unconditional love and commitment is not nurtured, running from responsibility becomes the first inclination, but it always leads to destruction. Rejected responsibility is the result of rejected love.

8. Devastated Dreams

If we begin marriage with hopes of grandeur, but neglect to evaluate our motives and interpersonal skills, eventually we'll become ensnared by the consequences that stem from the "me first" philosophy. No longer do we have time to dream of goals and ambitions; we become caught up in a day-to-day struggle to understand what has gone wrong. We all want good things to happen in marriage, but we must want them for the right reasons. It is not wrong to dream, indeed it is healthy, but in marriage dreams and desires are never solitary visions. Though their attainment may satisfy personal ambition, goals or dreams must be reached with the cooperation and support of a well-informed, participating partner.

Love demands that we involve our spouses. Dreams must never be attained at a spouse's expense. Too often the words "I need to go find myself" become the epitaph for a marriage ruined by individual pursuits. We must always remember that true love flourishes when we focus our efforts on the desires of our spouses rather than on our own desires. Spouse-centered living is a reflection of devotion, but a devastated marriage is a reflection of self-indulgence.

As a result of devastated dreams, marriage becomes a deadly game of romantic roulette. We marry, hoping to have all of our needs and desires met, only to become disillusioned by the inability of our spouses to satisfy our expectations. By focusing on what we will get from the relationship rather than what we will give, we depreciate our spouses and shatter our dreams.

Our future should be filled with dreams, plans that give life purpose and invigorate our day-to-day experience. Dreams give purpose and energy to the marriage marathon. Without them life becomes dull, tiring, and directionless, yet this is where much more than half of married couples find themselves. Without shared dreams, we struggle with our spouses, trying to determine when they changed, what they may have done wrong, why they seem so uncaring and uninvolved. Because dreams are not being considered and shared, we lose energy and vision, become jealous of others whose journeys appears more purposeful, and doubt whether or not it is possible to get to the finish line. Once our spouses cared and dreamed. Now those feelings are lost in routine and survival. Because of the lack of spouse-centered living and uncultivated skills, dreams for a satisfying tomorrow are gradually replaced by tedious and wearisome activities that are repeated day after monotonous day. Dreams give passion and focus to a relationship. They make the possibility of winning the marriage marathon real and reachable, and the ride to the finish line more invigorating.

9. Shattered Society

Though it may seem that the effects of a shattered society are not immediately relevant to marriage, we must not ignore them. Good marriages foster a strong society. Shattered homes lead to a shattered society. The whole is never stronger than the parts. Public values ultimately reflect private values. The church, government, and marriage are institutions that should promote love, selflessness, commitment, gentleness, patience, and peace. The characteristics inherent to a successful marriage are the same characteristics that give the church and government their strength.

Both church and state ultimately reflect the quality of the marriages within them. Successful marriages, directly or indirectly, are the proving grounds in which leaders develop and are prepared to serve society. If marriage fails to promote biblical principles, corruption in other institutions is inevitable. The choices we make in our marriages will reach far beyond our family to all of those with whom we have contact. How we relate to our spouses has consequences that can either enrich or devastate society for generations. Headlines in the future are based on the strength of a society's homes today.

A "Me First" Slippery Slope

As you reflect on the nine bitter fruits that result from ignoring your spouses' needs, notice the progression. One idea leads to the next, and the cumulative effect is devastating. Not much in life is more treacherous than racing a bike without brakes down a wet and winding course. This is what selfishness does to marriage: it leaves you out of control. It rains down nothing but tragedy and danger, which, left unchecked, will postpone or cancel participation in the marriage marathon. We don't intend for our marriages to slide downhill like this, but without conscious preventive effort, this is exactly what will happen.

Shifting Gears

Just as a cyclist shifts gears along the course to victory, individuals who desire a lasting marriage need to shift gears from self-centered to spouse-centered living. The following pages describe a principle and framework through which we can maintain a spouse-centered approach to life. Any couple who does not make this shift for the road ahead will drastically handicap their chances of completing the marriage journey. We must never become so focused on our individual goals, our personal satisfaction, or on our weariness, that we forget that a marriage-marathon bicycle is built for two, not one.

CHAPTER 2

A Bicycle Built for Two

The marriage marathon is a journey on which two individuals embark. Before marrying, however long ago that may have been, each of us traveled through life on the seat of a bicycle that was obedient to the wise and foolish inclinations of a single mind: our own. At the outset of the marriage marathon, each mind is immediately blessed with the intrusion—I mean inclusion—of a second mind.

This creates a few options. The couple can decide to stay on their individual bikes, each traveling at his or her own pace, making his or her own decisions, and handling upcoming hazards individually. The couple can choose to have one spouse ride side saddle, which places the other spouse in the position of being the primary decision maker. An extra degree of risk is added to the journey when only one person is involved in making decisions. Another option is to purchase a bicycle that will allow the couple to share the responsibilities of the journey, while protecting and assisting each other and creating a more rewarding journey throughout the marriage marathon. The solution that gives the most dividends appears to be the purchase of a tandem bicycle—a bicycle built for two.

The Right Equipment

During the preparation period before marriage, a couple meet, court one another, and eventually marry, each believing to have found that "special person." Often the excitement of the marriage day reflects the importance of what may be seen as the crowning event in our brief experience together. In reality, this day marks only the beginning of a journey that carries with it many surprises that could not possibly have been foreseen. We often make the mistake of assuming that we know the person we married better than anyone we have ever known.

Whether this belief is true or not, time has a way of bringing events into our lives that challenge us and awaken us to weaknesses and attitudes never seen in our spouses—or in ourselves. It's sort of like realizing that, though married, we are riding separate bicycles, and the separation between us is growing greater.

Some differences in marriage exist because one person is male and the other female. How these differences are going to play out over time cannot be predicted. If you aren't aware of these gender differences, your spouse's reaction to a given situation can be completely baffling.

There is also the baggage that is brought into the marriage: all that emotional and mental stuff collected from extended families and during the single years (or any previous marriage). We come into the marriage with a history. Whether this history is known or unknown to our spouses, there is no way to determine how it will play out over the ensuing years. Marriage is a lifelong challenge to get to know oneself, but even more important, it is a commitment to gain a deeper understanding of one's partner.

Though we all begin marriage with some degree of love for our partners, the depth of this love is questionable simply because we do not have an adequate understanding of our spouses' healthy and unhealthy histories. Without that knowledge, we can't sufficiently meet the challenge of the commitment to our own innate, but inexperienced love. It is difficult to fully love someone about whom one, in reality, knows very little.

As time passes, challenges will confront the love that is held for a spouse. Do the revelations or surprises create a desire to know and understand more fully the unique people we have married, or do they cause us to feed our disappointments with doubts about the decision to marry? When doubts come, the true quality and depth of our love is being revealed to us. If we can learn from the surprises that engender differences in and unexpected changes to our lives, love will grow stronger. The hope of love begins a relationship; knowledge of one another challenges love's sincerity and commitment. Acquiring a "bicycle built for two" mentality helps a couple face each other's personal history, gender differences, and those occasional surprises together.

Riding a Bicycle Built for Two

The statement that "it takes two to fight" is true. But in marriage, it only takes one person to turn the dream of a good marriage into a nasty nightmare. The idea that a married couple is "one flesh" is true in the positional sense of the word, but in practice, a couple spends their entire journey throughout life shaping and perfecting their one-flesh union. When two individuals decide to "team up" to ride a tandem bicycle in a marathon, on paper—or positionally—they are a team, a union. Practically they are as separate as the day they made their decision. Time, together with the development and practice of a strategy that commits both to dedicate their energy to the success the other, will mold them into a single unit.

The same is true in marriage. If oneness or intimacy in a practical sense is to be realized, we must commit to a strategy that places the needs of our spouses before our own, and our spouses must do the same. It is important to understand how we can place the needs of our spouses before our own without being used and abused.

The Needs Cycle

Many have heard of the philosophy that marriage is a fifty-fifty proposition. It sounds something like this: "If one spouse gives 50 percent and the other gives 50 percent, a union can be achieved." Actually this formula can only create a union divided. If an employer hires two people and requests that these two employees give 100 percent, that employer expects 100 percent from both individuals. If the two employees get together and contrive a plan based on a fifty-fifty philosophy, their employer's calculations of their productivity will not be met. They will each fall short by 50 percent. Each employee must give 100 percent to the job if the potential of their labor is to be reached.

Such is the case in marriage. Both spouses must commit to giving 100 percent to the welfare of the marriage. If they want to experience the potential of their union, they must devote their full energy to it, nothing withheld. People fearful of total commitment often hold divorce as a ready option. By eliminating the possibility of divorce we free our marriages from the threat of separation and the fear of participation. We must focus on the needs of our spouses first, rather than on our own. If we commit to this principle, any solutions and suggestions we offer will always be sympathetic to and include the opinions and concerns of our spouses. This policy is not always easy to put into practice on a daily basis, but it is less traumatic than running off the marriage course and crashing into the consequences of divorce.

Meeting each other's needs is a *responsibility,* not an *option*. It is the couple's responsibility to help their marriage reach its fullest potential by focusing on the intellectual, physical, emotional, sexual, and spiritual needs of the other. Each spouse shares the same responsibility. When each spouse follows this course, the natural tendency to focus on oneself is lessened, and each develops a sense of healthy interdependence with the other that produces stability and security. Each is convinced daily of the other's loyalty and value to the relationship. This is the process and purpose of the Needs Cycle.

Because meeting each other's needs is critical to the growth and stability of a marriage, it is imperative that we communicate our needs, wants, and desires clearly. To do otherwise is to place a spouse in a no-win situation. We cannot expect spouses to meet needs of which they are unaware. Though many needs can be learned by attending a seminar or by reading material on marriage, the best way to be certain that our spouses understand our needs is to tell them.

What determines our needs? Throughout our lives, we all need the bare necessities of air, food, and shelter. But there is much more to human need than these physical elements because we are not merely physical beings; we are creatures created in the image of God with the capacity to think, will, and feel. Our fallen or sinful nature creates needs for us that we would not have had in an unfallen world. The need to accomplish something of value or have purpose and the need to love and be loved were fully satisfied until human sin altered God's original condition for us. Humanity's purpose and love for one another was originally complete because we were living in obedience to the Creator (cf. Gen. 1:26–2:25). Once disobedience entered the pristine environment of creation, we became needy people. What we became spiritually forced relational needs upon us that transcend the physical needs of air, food, and shelter. When we broke up with God, we broke up with one another. Only when we reconnect with God through obedience will we be able to find lasting purpose and love (John 15:8–17) and relationships that matter and last.[1]

It is logical to assume that our relational needs are intrinsically connected to the relationship we have with God. If our spouses, for any reason, are unable to meet our relational needs over an extended period of time, can we assume that a good relationship with God will suffice to overcome the physical, emotional, sexual, or intellectual losses? Ultimately the answer is yes because we can do all things through Christ who strengthens us (Phil. 4:13) and all things do work together for good to those who love God (Rom. 8:28). But how does God work out the difficulties that stem from unmet needs? We would like to suggest that this process includes the presence of people whom God brings into our lives.

God places people in our lives who meet relational needs such as feeling valued and loved. In marriage, the person God chooses is your spouse! God did not design us to have our relationship needs met through Him alone. When He created Adam, God said, "It is not good for man to be alone; I will make him a helper suitable for him" (Gen. 2:18). Spouses have responsibilities before God to meet one another's needs. Just as a tandem racing team needs each other to succeed, spouses need one another to succeed. If one or the other forgets to consider the needs of the other, disappointment will ensue.

Though God will never forsake us and will provide a way of escape when temptation confronts us (1 Cor. 10:13), the pain and suffering that we must endure because real needs are being ignored stems from a spouse's failure to fulfill divinely decreed responsibilities (Eph. 5:21–33). Our relationship with God determines the quality of our devotion to the other, our "needs meeting" capability. Therefore, the degree to which we meet the needs of our spouses determines the relational wellness of our spouses and our marriages. Success in the marriage marathon demands the involvement and commitment of both God and each spouse if real love is to be achieved. The moral obligation for meeting human needs cannot be placed solely in the hands of the Lord. Every individual has an essential part to play in the success or failure of any society or relationship.

A Word of Caution

To accept a philosophy of meeting one another's needs carries great responsibility and personal risk. If one spouse does not commit to practicing the Needs Cycle, manipulation and frustration are inevitable. For example, if a wife focuses on the needs of her husband while he simply enjoys her efforts, eventually his lack of commitment to his wife will become apparent. Because her needs are not being meet, she will become drained to the point of having to focus on her own needs to survive, or else be of no more value than an empty Gatorade bottle whose nourishment went to her husband. It is critical that both partners commit their total energy to meeting each other's needs in order to prevent the weakening and eventual emotional or physical division of their union. As we focus on the needs of our spouses, we protect ourselves from the natural inclination toward selfishness and the painful consequences that accompany it. The danger of riding tandem becomes most threatening when one rider decides to ride independently of, or without concern for, the other.

Temporary Need-Stoppers

The attempt to meet each other's needs 100 percent of the time is a goal every couple should strive to achieve. Even if it is a difficult ideal, it should not be abandoned because of its challenge. The fruits from the effort far outweigh the difficulty it takes to obtain them. However, as we strive to meet each other's needs, certain responsibilities arise that demand our attention. These responsibilities sometimes force us to expend extra time and energy that limits the focus we can place on our spouses' needs.

What is disconcerting about these "temporary need-stoppers" is that they have the potential of not being temporary; we can become so involved in them that we focus on them at the expense of our spouses. They must remain what their name states: temporary. They are to be given necessary attention in order to prevent them from overshadowing the primary responsibility to meet the needs of the spouse. You may need to take some personal time, for instance, to read for intellectual stimulation, but too much time away from your partner is dangerous. Don't forget that your primary responsibility is to meet the needs of your spouse. You and your spouse are one and, therefore, cannot last long without the support of the other. To focus too long on other responsibilities (human or otherwise) starves the marriage union of the necessary relational nutrients (love, honor, and encouragement; see strategy two) that make winning the marriage marathon possible. The prolonged emotional or physical absence of one spouse may result in the emotional or physical wandering of the other spouse. Eventually the other spouse might choose to find a more "focused" rider.

Career/Vocation

Often we become frustrated with the amount of time our jobs take from our marriages. Many couples fail to consider what the role of a vocation or career is in the larger context of their marriages. Often this is because people view their vocation as something separate from their marriage, when in fact the two are intricately connected. Unfortunately too many individuals perceive work as a personal identity issue, that is, an opportunity to succeed and make a statement about their personal worth. Others seek employment, which they hope they will enjoy, because they know they need to do it to support their spouses and families.

Though it is not inherently wrong to seek employment that will bring personal satisfaction, we must ultimately define our reason for working in relation to this question: "Do we work for our own interests or for the interests of our families?" How we answer this question will determine the amount of extra time we focus on the job, the attitudes with which we handle family concerns and the difficulties that accompany any job, and the priority a career takes in relation to our spouses. A couple can better tolerate or support each other's vocations when each partner is assured that the time devoted to a job is, in reality, time devoted to the couple's union or family.

Low Self-Esteem

In a society that promotes happiness as the quintessential quality of one's life, sorrow and disappointment can easily create discouragement and depression. No one can be happy all the time, and we would question the mental state of somebody who was that way. Perpetual happiness is unrealistic in a fallen world and in a society where bad things inevitably happen to good people. In fact, low self-esteem or mild cases of depression are often warning signs that the body needs a change or is tired and needs rest. Often after a great achievement, people experience bouts with depression. It is normal and it passes with time, rest, encouragement, education, and reentry into one's normal life. When we are concerned about the welfare and needs of our spouses, it is reasonable to give, and he or she will welcome, a word of encouragement, time for rest, and acceptance of bouts with disappointment.[2]

Low self-esteem becomes a problem when it goes unchecked and overcoming it becomes the focal point around which the marriage revolves. If a cyclist is weakening from dehydration, the partner responds to the immediate need by making sure that thirst is quenched. Otherwise it will not be long before the racers make an unfortunate turn for the worse. Low self-esteem is an understandable experience that temporarily demands the focus of both partners on the one who is hurting in order to ensure individual recovery so that the needs of both can be met.

Low self-esteem is best resolved by doing something good for someone else—anything that you know honors the Lord. Accomplishments, no matter the size, produce confidence that boosts self-esteem. So if you or your spouse is feeling a bit down, identify the problem, respect each other's perspective on the issue, and then do something special for each other. You may not be able to solve the problem immediately, but doing something considerate for each other keeps discouragement at bay and helps remind both of you about what is most important—your marriage union.

Children

Too often parents believe that their children's needs are more important than the needs of the marriage. Nothing is farther from the truth. Children learn the value of marriage through parents who love and honor each other above everyone and everything else. This does not mean that the needs of the children are unimportant, for indeed they are. Often, especially in the toddler and infant years, the needs of these more dependent children require greater attention. Sometimes this attention does not allow us the time we need with our spouses. But we must never ignore our spouses' needs for an extended period of time. When children are brought into the family, they become a part of it, not its focus! The stronger the relationship between the parents, the more well adjusted the children.[3]

Illness

When we become ill, a loving spouse jumps in to fill the gap, understanding that his or her own needs will be temporarily unmet. Unfortunately, some people actually are offended if their partners become ill because it interrupts their schedule. This is a clear sign that selfishness has a strong root system in the lives of such persons.

Because our spouses must take on extra responsibilities when we are ill, it is important that we take the necessary steps to return to full health if possible. When we don't follow medical advise, we create an unnecessary burden on our care-giving spouses because we usually don't get better as quickly and this extends the time that his or her needs will go unmet.

If an illness or injury is extensive (such as cancer, chronic illness, or a debilitating accident), real love demands extreme measures. It may be that a permanent injury or a life-threatening disease makes it impossible for us to meet our partners' needs. At this point the focus of a marriage changes, especially the expectations spouses have of one another. If we *cannot* meet a need, the disappointment from the loss is lessened because expectations change. The Needs Cycle continues (see pages 41–43), but with expectations that are consistent with the capabilities of the ill spouse. As we age, the reality of decreased capabilities becomes more telling! Love stays the course to ensure that all those dependent on it are safe and supported. Please remember that success in the marriage marathon involves how we negotiate the journey so that we finish together. The marriage marathon is not concerned with placing first.

Premenstrual Syndrome (PMS)

Generally speaking, women of childbearing years experience menstruation monthly. Many women experience slight to severe physical and emotional changes in connection with menstruation. These women have what is known as premenstrual tension or syndrome (PMS). "It is estimated that 90 percent of all women have some degree of premenstrual tension, and probably one-third of all menstruating women have a full-blown case of PMS."[4] During this time, it is essential that the husband put his needs on the shelf and help his wife. It is a temporary inconvenience that should act as a monthly reminder of the struggle women experience as the "life-givers to humanity." Life is preserved through suffering that lasts throughout the childbearing years. This uniquely female experience should cause a husband to respect his wife and give to her the honor and support she needs and deserves.

The Broken Needs Cycle

What happens if a spouse's needs go unmet for extended periods of time? When working with couples, counselors hear numerous remarks that clearly indicate the Needs Cycle is not being maintained. Once in a while, a frustrated spouse will say, "I don't love him/her anymore; I guess I never did." In many cases this is a true statement. Often the challenges of married life reveal the true commitment of those who embraced its journey for other than pure motives. Meeting the needs of their spouse wasn't a consideration: they married for status, out of responsibility, in ignorance of the guidelines, or because their partner was socially acceptable. Without intervention, the consequence is a humiliating divorce or, at best, a miserable marriage. In other cases, the statement reflects a love that has been drained while one partner tried to do his or her part without any help from the spouse. It is difficult to keep loving someone who takes your love and gives nothing in return. Sometimes a family pet is more supportive instinctively than some spouses are intentionally!

Another clue that the Needs Cycle is broken is when a client says, "He doesn't show any interest in me anymore." When people's needs are not being met, they naturally attempt to get those needs met somewhere else or through other interests. This statement doesn't make it immediately clear which spouse is neglecting the other or whether both are guilty, but it certainly reveals that needs are being ignored and the path on which the couple is riding is becoming more tenuous.

"She seems uninterested in making love." Sexual fulfillment is one of the first things to go when a woman's emotional and intellectual needs are being ignored. No one wants to be intimate with a person who wants the benefits of a marital relationship without the responsibility that shapes it. It is also possible that the wife may not have clearly expressed her needs and is resentful that they are not being met. Remember that people are not mind readers; a spouse won't automatically know your needs because he or she loves you!

Spouses who find home life a place where their opinions are belittled or where they are constantly berated for doing things wrong with the kids may accept overtime work at their jobs as an alternative to going home. They may even want to join another softball team or another social club. At least at work or with their friends, their needs for respect and friendship are being met. When a spouse doesn't come home after work to spend time with the family, it may be that there is no encouragement to do so. No one wants to be in an environment that is demeaning or where one's opinions or needs are made light of. From the outset of marriage, we should spend more time identifying things for which to praise one another; it is easy to spot the negatives and focus on disappointments, but doing so creates disunion and does nothing toward helping us reach our potential.

One of the most distressing things to hear from a client is the statement, "I guess it was never meant to be." Those words of despair imply that one or both spouses is considering giving up. While the other statements we've discussed are more or less true, this statement is utterly false. It may be understandable that someone could feel despair, nonetheless, it is false to assume that a marriage was never meant to be. Couples who fail to meet one another's needs leave their hopes and dreams on a courtroom floor or hanging like useless old clothes in the closet of a cold, sterile marriage. Couples who find that their marriages have gone awry often mistakenly believe that they made mistakes in choosing partners. They believe they are in a marriage that cannot succeed. Yet the truth is that *everyone's marriage is meant to be.*

The question is: do couples possess the skills and understanding to keep their marriages alive? Many do not, or if they do, they don't apply them. When spouses don't focus on each other's needs, they leave each other destined to desire another more "compatible partner" with whom they can journey through the marriage marathon in a more meaningful way. Spouses must learn about each other's differences so they can understand and meet each other's needs.

CHAPTER 3

Know Who
Else Is Peddling!

*R*iding tandem requires that riders know as much as they can about one another. It means they need to know each other's physical strengths and limitations and their emotional stamina under pressure. Their detailed knowledge of one another not only helps them overcome the odds that threaten to disqualify them but also defines the parameters within which each rider operates in order to assist and support the other as they pursue their mutual goal—completing the course together.

The marriage marathon requires no less. We must commit to studying and understanding each other's physical, emotional, sexual, and spiritual differences. These differences, if acknowledged, give us awareness of the complexities that create a unique, special—though imperfect—partner. Awareness of differences makes the journey special as we work together for one another's care and benefit. Ignorance of differences creates unnecessary hazards that eventually force us to look out for ourselves at the expense of our spouses. It is better to know the person who peddles through life with you than to wonder each day what road he or she might take on the trail ahead.

Physical Differences

The most obvious differences between men and women are physical. But the effect these differences have on behavior is not always so clear. It is important that we recognize and learn to appreciate our physical differences. They help us understand our spouses' physical strengths and weaknesses, which make us aware of his or her specific needs.[1] Geneticist Anne Moir and journalist David Jessel wrote:

Men are different from women. They are equal only in their common membership of the same species, humankind. To maintain that they are the same in aptitude, skill or behavior is to build a society based on a biological and scientific lie. . . . Men and women could live more happily, understand and love each other better, organize the world to better effect, if we acknowledged our differences. We could then build our lives on the twin pillars of our distinct sexual identities. It is time to cease the vain contention that men and women are created the same. They were not, and no amount of idealism or Utopian fantasy can alter the fact. It can only strain the relationship between the sexes.[2]

Women and men are created equally in the image of God, but they are also created individually and uniquely as men and as women. The physical differences between men and women include varying amounts of the same hormones, various metabolic rates (the rate at which the body consumes energy), distinct and differing susceptibilities to disease, and individual endurance levels based upon particular respiratory systems and muscle mass.[3] Within each marriage, these differences play a major part in determining the activities in which a couple engages. Without an adequate understanding and acceptance of your spouse's physical potential, it is easy to expect more of your spouse than he or she is physically able to accomplish. Physical differences should remind us that partners may not be able to run the race at the same pace, but it is critical that both spouses remain in the race. Too often in the marriage marathon, one spouse's lack of knowledge regarding the physical differences of the other results in unnecessary and lonely separations throughout the course. Going the distance together requires a mutual understanding of each other's abilities and limitations, agreement on a realistic and shared pace, and the willingness to adjust to each other's abilities and limitations, thus creating a uniquely cohesive and comfortable union—your marriage!

Have you set aside a time to focus on the particular physical attributes and characteristics that define your spouse? Are you aware of your spouse's physical concerns and desires? Do they matter to you? They should! You can't love or meet your spouse's needs without having the answers to these questions. It is a human duty to apply one's skills, physical or otherwise, to meet the needs of others, *especially* one's spouse. Superiority, inferiority, and equality issues should have nothing to do with physical differences. Rather, these differences identify roles that are created to protect society, not subjugate its more weaker or handicapped members. In issues that matter in the world of relationships, it is important to know that husbands and wives have physical differences that create different needs. Whatever those differences are, they need to be identified so that faulty expectations are not created and real needs are met.[4] Never allow physical differences that surface over the life of your marriage to cause relational deterioration or to detract from the ultimate goal of your marriage, which is finishing the journey together.

Emotional Differences

When it comes to emotional differences, men *tend* to lean more toward the characteristics of a bull while women *tend* to behave like a bumblebee. What do we mean by this? Basic emotional differences exist between *most* men and women, though there is certainly some overlap. Men tend to be more aggressive, impersonal, and less emotional than women. Women tend to be more personal, more interactive, and more sensitive to the needs and emotional temperature of others. Gathering information from one spot to the next, in the same way that a bumblebee gathers pollen from one flower to the next, they provide themselves with a network for deeper relationships.[5]

Women Place a High Priority on Intimacy

Another word for intimacy is oneness. Knowledge about the lives of the people a woman cares about is important to her in developing what she sees as a strong relationship. The less she knows about a person, the less close her relationship with that person is. Just as a bee goes from plant to plant, a woman goes from issue to issue, gathering information that gives her a greater knowledge of a person with whom she desires friendship or simply peaceful coexistence, as in a workplace. Her friendships are strengthened and maintained by a network of interaction and information. So what about men?

Men Focus on Identity, Independence, and Career

What a man owns and does has a lot to do with how he feels about himself. Knowledge of the personal lives of those he works with is often inconsequential; however, his ability to do what he does is everything.

Men also like to feel that they can do what they do with minimal assistance. Directions are often viewed as a necessary nuisance; a man will toil in isolation until he masters a task and can proudly say, "Yeah, I know how to do that." Men tend to have fewer friends, but when they establish a friendship, it can last a lifetime. Most men are not comfortable being vulnerable, so when they decide to open up, they do so cautiously. They don't want to appear weak in any context.

Women Are Much More Personal

Women are much more comfortable building relationships. Vulnerability is not as great a threat because they desire to know people and be known. However, a wounded woman who has been betrayed can carry an awful sting.

This personal or relational quality of women can be seen both at home and in the workplace. A woman is much more prone to make the workplace a "home away from home" complete with plants, pictures, and souvenirs from family vacations. Generally, she prefers her office to be kept tidy in the same way that her home is kept. Her environment reflects greatly on how she wants to be perceived. Often when a husband places a dirty garment in a place other than a laundry basket, it is taken as a personal offense. A woman's home and workplace are an extension of who she is.

Men Are More Impersonal

Men are fairly lineal and goal oriented. The quickest way to get from point "A" to point "B" is a straight line. If that path happens to break a few dishes (or hearts) on the way, it's too bad, but the job has to be done. It is somewhat like a bull in a china shop. It's not that men don't like people; they just don't have a need to know anyone who isn't directly linked with what they are doing. They are goal oriented or solution driven. The more they get done, the better they believe they are at what they do. "Show me the quantifiable facts."

This explains why men love statistics and why sports stations constantly put them on the screen. They love to win; this means— hopefully in a lighthearted way—that people are tools through which victory can be achieved. Men like people, but in the heat of battle, others have to lose. As long as men care about others and maintain values of human dignity, these characteristics are mostly fun and help them accomplish goals; however, when selfishness or ignorance of others' needs set in, this quality can turn ugly and uncaring. In a real sense, it is helpful for men to strive to be more like women in how they handle relationships.

Earlier, we noted that men are stronger physically; emotionally, however, women have the edge. In a marriage marathon, men need to remember that success doesn't imply outdoing the Joneses in the number of romantic dates a year or having a nicer home than the Smith family. The marriage marathon is a relationship that involves knowledge and commitment throughout a long journey. It is not always a fast-paced rush to victory; more often it's a steady dose of caring and reflection with pauses to reconsider strategy and shortcomings.

Women Express Anger More Verbally

Women, not being as physical as men, tend to unleash their anger verbally. Because men tend to express their anger physically by pushing, hitting, or breaking things, it is very important that spouses learn to respect this dangerous difference. Spouse abuse and violence is *always* wrong and is never justifiable by either party. Verbal abuse is as destructive as physical abuse, though not as deadly. Both must be stopped. The unleashing of anger never made anybody more secure in a relationship. Most of the anger spouses fling at each other comes from selfish attitudes that they are unwilling to control and change. We must see our spouses as more valuable than we see ourselves. We must place them on a pedestal that makes their growth more important than ours. In so doing, we create the possibility for our own growth through the support that naturally comes from the one we chose to cherish before ourselves.

To be close to his wife, a husband must be open and vulnerable. To be close to her husband, a wife must support and encourage him, especially in his profession. No matter how nonrelational a man might be, if he desires peace with his wife, he must improve in this area. The benefits will not only come to him, but to his wife, children, friends, and coworkers.[6]

Sexual Differences

Sexual differences have great impact on the success of the marriage marathon. Humans are sexual creatures by design, though we do have trouble differentiating between passion and lust. Men and women have strong sexual desires, but they look at sex from different perspectives.

To ignore or miss these differences can cause wounds that are difficult to heal. In marriage, the sex act carries with it a great deal of trust and loyalty; never think that it is the foundation of a good marriage and never take it for granted. It is blissfully satisfying on one end of a continuum, blisteringly searing at the other end. It ebbs and flows with the quality of a couple's relationship.

Men and Testosterone

Men have ten times as much testosterone as women. This fact often makes the behavior of many men very confusing to women. The male sex drive is fueled by a hormone that turns the most mild-mannered man into quite the aggressive sort when confined in a quiet locale with the wife of his dreams. Testosterone is like an unstable bottle of nitroglycerin. Bump it and it could explode; mix it with the right ingredients and a chemical reaction is sure to ensue. Women are often bewildered by the way their men can wake up in the morning, gaze at their wife beside them, whose breath is less than desirable and whose hair is more than a little disheveled, and still be sexually stimulated. The pure and simple fact is that testosterone builds while the body rests: Testosterone is at its highest level at sunrise.

What is even more incredible is the experience many wives face after enduring a *Rambo*-type movie with their husbands. After watching blood and guts for two hours, the man turns to his wife and drools with a pathetic passionate grin that makes the wife think her husband is a cannibal. Testosterone is stimulated by violence. Within seconds after a marital spat, a husband may want to "make up" with his emotionally scarred wife. He wrongly believes that sexual intercourse will help him and his wife forget the unpleasantness of their spat.

Some wives don't mind their husbands playing in intramural athletic events. That's fine, but such wives need to be sure to pray that their husbands don't join winning teams, or else they need to remember to keep track of the evenings their husbands play and prepare for romance. Testosterone responds well to victory.

Many husbands work out regularly. This is great for the cardiovascular system, but it also gives the testosterone a lift! You may wonder if there is anything a man can do that does not increase his testosterone level. Well hold that thought, because there is one more thing that causes a man's testosterone to rocket. Just looking at his wife causes him unbelievable excitement, especially when she dons his favorite dress for a special evening out. Men are visually stimulated. Unless you are one of the minority of women who have an extra dose of testosterone in your system, you might feel a bit overwhelmed. Because men are greatly influenced by their testosterone levels, they need to intentionally focus on becoming more relationally oriented. They need to take into account the things that stimulate their wives sexually so that their own sexual passion does not become offensive or abusive.[7]

Women and a Loving Touch

A woman, being relationally oriented, is stimulated more by the kindness and loving touch of her husband. For this reason, sexual stimulation is not always immediate or spontaneous.[8] It develops over a period of time; she is actually wooed by the sincerity and openness of her husband. For men, it seems to be a "look and leap" procedure; for women, it's "listen and learn." Men and women are very different sexually. If we do not want to injure each other, we must be sensitive to what stimulates our spouses. A husband cannot expect to be sexually intimate with his wife when he has been distant from or indifferent to her. A wife cannot expect her husband to be in her presence and not be sexually stimulated; it is always just a matter of time. To keep the sexual aspect of marriage healthy, both spouses must initially remain committed to the welfare of the other in the relational areas of their lives. Sexual intimacy is the culmination of a great day or week together. It cannot be expected in an environment that is uncaring and insensitive.

The Sex Drive

Men reach their sexual prime around the age of eighteen, while women reach their prime sometime in their thirties.[9] If a young man is unaware of this fact, his wife's apparent lack of interest may cause him to think she is seeing someone else, doesn't love him, or is not attracted to him. Most of the time the problem may lie in the development of the different sex drives. Other times the problem may be that his wife has an unusually low level of testosterone; sexual excitement does not come easily for these women. Still other women may have suffered from incest or another form of sexual abuse. Men who marry women who have suffered from these violent acts will have to make adjustments that are consistent with their vows: in sickness and in health. Some women are never able to fully recover sexually from violent acts perpetrated against them. These women need compassionate husbands to show them the true meaning of sacrificial love as they continue to recover from their past ordeals. Often this recovery requires professional counseling and sensitive pastoral care.

Sex is wonderful, but it is not the ultimate expression of true love. Crossing the finish line is exhilarating, but preparation and staying power makes success possible. The quality of a couple's relationship defines the quality of their sexuality.

Men and Marriage

Men tend to marry because of physical and erotic attraction, and they hopefully develop a deeper relationship with their spouse after the wedding. That may sound like an awful commentary on men, but all too often this seems to be the case. The experience of relationship does not come easy for men. This means that many men marry for selfish motives—a foundation that can't withstand the demands of a lifelong marriage. If they fail to become more relational and other-centered, such men find marriage frustrating and suffocating. However, when they do become relational, they develop comfort and peace in the hearts of their wives and in themselves. Marriage is a relationship that is built on courtesy and cooperation, not on wants and fantasies. An entrepreneur can't incorporate a business and then expect the company to work on its own. Benefits or profits are gained through commitment, understanding what employees need to reach their greatest potential, and creating an environment conducive to collaboration. The same is true in marriage.

Women and Marriage

Because women are more relational, they tend to grasp the concept of "selfless love" much more quickly. They marry wanting to develop a relationship with a man whose actual courtship skills usually reveal less depth relationally than what appears on the surface. Women are interested in understanding a man who comforts them, and they hope that they have found the one with whom they can share their innermost feelings and thoughts. Too often the husband squelches this marvelous sensitivity and vulnerability at the outset of marriage. For far too many men, the relationship skills used during the courting years are part of their competitive effort to "bag," or capture, the women who have stirred their testosterone. After the wedding, the openness that was so prevalent during the courting years dissipates. After all, he has won his trophy. Ten years ago, Gary memorized a statement that has not left him to this day: "If a marriage is experiencing marital difficulty after five years, it is safe to assume that the problem lies primarily with the husband."[10] He didn't agree with this comment at the time, but over the years, its truth has been fixed in his mind. Men must learn sensitivity to people's feelings, experience the trust that comes from risking vulnerability, and never lose the heart that sees courting as the continual winning of one's wife throughout the marriage marathon.

Spiritual Differences

The source that determines the guidelines for a successful marathon is the race committee. The source who determines the guidelines for a successful marriage is the Person who designed the institution of marriage. That person is God, the Creator. We are told at the close of the creation story that God designed marriage to be an inseparable union between one man and one woman (Gen. 2:18–25). In the beginning, not even death could separate Adam and Eve's union because both were immortal and without sin, completely open and honest with God and one another. It wasn't long, however, before the first couple yielded to temptation. Their fall away from God resulted in self-centeredness, egoism, and mortality. Without the Fall, there would be no concern about spiritual differences between men and women who marry; because of the Fall, however, spiritual differences exist and must be understood. The spiritual health and maturity of each partner within a marriage has impact on not only the manner in which the marriage marathon is conducted but carries implications that extend well beyond the completion of the marriage marathon.

Peddling in Different Directions

When it comes to choosing a spouse, too often emotions and physical attraction take precedence over faith. Couples assume that their "love" for one another will overcome the spiritual differences between them. This *may* be the case if neither couple has any serious commitment to his or her faith. For couples who express faith in Christ, however, spiritual compatibility forms the foundation on which the marriage unions rests and from which the commitments (strategies) remain intact throughout the marriage marathon.

Couples can be physically, emotionally, and sexually different from one another without those differences jeopardizing their marriage, but spiritual differences are directly related to maturity. Spiritual maturity measures the difference (gap) between how much a person lives according to the flesh and how much a person lives according to the Holy Spirit's guidance (Gal. 5:16–26). Spiritual immaturity on the part of one or both spouses leads to jealousy, division, and eventually to unteachableness (1 Cor. 3:1–11; Heb. 5:11–14). Partners in a marriage must continually narrow the spiritual gap between them as they strive together to narrow the spiritual gap between themselves and their God (Eph. 3:17–19). The narrower the gap (the fewer the differences), the stronger the relationship. Righteousness is the fruit of spiritual maturity and is the character that strengthens relationships (cf. Job 17:9; Ps. 84:5–7; Prov. 4:18). The more like God we become, the more able we are to love our spouses, honor our commitments, and, therefore, win the marriage marathon.

Understanding and accepting differences that are physical, emotional, and sexual in nature help couples to love and care for one another even when those differences cannot be changed; but understanding differences that are spiritual in nature must always lead each partner to change (spiritual growth) so that the service of each to the other and to their God is good and acceptable (Rom. 12:1–2). Oneness of faith makes oneness of union everything it is intended to be. Remember that marriage is God's institution—to fully experience the wonder of the one-flesh relationship, a couple must pursue oneness with God (true spirituality).

Spiritual differences between believers and unbelievers make the journey through marriage more of a challenge. If you are unmarried, do not pursue a relationship with a person of a different faith than you. It is possible for two people to love and care for one another (follow the strategies of the marriage marathon) while professing different faiths, but the possibility for disappointment and failure is high. Trust God to know best how to join two people into one, and note that He prohibits marriages between believers and unbelievers (2 Cor. 6:14–18).

If you are a believer and are presently married to an unbeliever, or have come to Christ after marrying an unbeliever, or are a believer who is married to a believer who has chosen to neglect his or her faith, we encourage you to read 1 Corinthians 7:10–17 and 1 Peter 3:1–2, 7–9, and then consult your pastor or a very theologically grounded Christian counselor. Also, please continue reading *Winning the Marriage*

Marathon. Your marriage is unique, and knowing how to put it on course will help you to love your spouse in such a way that he or she will come to appreciate your commitment and loyalty to the marriage. The spiritual differences between you and your spouse will cause a few bumps along the way, but give the Lord time to work. If your spouse chooses to leave, you are not required to hold on to the relationship, but if your spouse desires to remain and love and care for you, stay with the marriage and pursue your faith in Christ.

Peddling in the Same Direction

Genesis 1:26–27 says, "Then God said, 'Let Us make man in Our image, according to Our likeness; let them have dominion . . . over all the earth. . . . So God created man in His own image, in the image of God He created him; male and female He created them'" (NKJV). As images of God, we have been blessed with authority from God and have the privilege of representing Him before others. As married partners, each of you is to represent Him to the other, and your union is to represent His will and character to all who see and know you. This is an incredible responsibility that you must never take lightly. You are examples of His plan for marriage, not humanity's plan for marriage. You are also a ray of hope, a light in the darkness to a world that desperately needs more examples of genuine love and commitment. After your oath to God, your oath to one another becomes the greatest commitment you will every make. Enjoy the blessings and benefits that a union blessed by God is entitled to, but do not forget that your marriage has a higher responsibility and goal, and that is to portray, as clearly as possible, a picture of God's impeccable will and character, and more specifically, His undying love to those who call Him Lord.

As Christians, we are to submit ourselves to one another and always be concerned for one another's welfare. But there is a specific role within marriage that God has designed that depicts not only His own relationships within the Trinity or Godhead, but also depicts the genuine love that takes place between God and His children, the church. *Marriage is given the privilege of being a human example of divine love and commitment.* (Note the similes—comparisons—joined by "as" in Eph. 5:22–33.)

> [22]Wives, submit to your own husbands, as to the Lord. [23]For the husband is head of the wife, as also Christ is head of

the church; and He is the Savior of the body. [24]Therefore, just as the church is subject to Christ, so let the wives be to their own husbands in everything. [25]Husbands, love your wives, just as Christ also loved the church and gave Himself for it, [26]that He might sanctify and cleanse it with the washing of water by the word, [27]that He might present it to Himself a glorious church, not having spot or wrinkle or any such thing, but that it should be holy and without blemish. [28]So husbands ought to love their own wives as their own bodies; *he who loves his wife loves himself.* [29]For no one ever hated his own flesh, but nourishes and cherishes it, just as the Lord does the church. [30]For we are members of His body, of His flesh and of His bones. [31]"For this reason a man shall leave his father and mother and be joined to his wife, and the two shall become one flesh." [32]This is a great mystery, but I speak concerning Christ and the church. [33]Nevertheless let each one of you in particular so love his own wife as himself, and let the wife see that she respects her husband. (NKJV, emphasis added)

Notice how much space is given to instruct the wife and how much is given to instruct the husband (three and a half verses address the wife, eight and a half verses address the husband). As the example of divine love to the world, it is critical that the husband understands his role. He is not a dominator or controller; he is a caregiver and protector who would sacrifice his very life for that of his wife. The role of the wife becomes a relatively simple matter when it operates in relation to a husband who loves in this manner, that is, as Christ loves. The man and the woman have become one flesh; it is inconceivable that the husband would or could even injure or hurt his own body, of which she is a part. As believers are one with Christ, so two individuals who marry are one with one another. It should not be startling to us that the world thinks these roles are strange, for everything about God is strange to the world. What is disappointing is that this understanding of the marriage relationship is strange to believers.

As partners who continue peddling in the same direction, remember: never take your eyes off the Lord. He is the light that clears your path and brings you joy. To forsake the Lord is to forsake one another, so never stop growing in your faith. Also, don't underestimate the cunning tenacity of Satan and his world to diminish your love for one another through familiarity and busyness. No matter how difficult the journey may get, respond to each situation with the interest of your spouse in mind. Only couples who desire to reflect the character of Jesus Christ in their marriage can produce genuine meaning that leads to eternal reward. A marriage that clings to the Lord's principles will not fail; indeed, it cannot fail. It is our prayer that your marriage will be a testimony of the love, commitment, and patient endurance of Jesus Christ to all who know you.

CHAPTER 4

Winning the Race Together

*O*nce we identify the differences between spouses, we can identify the needs that those differences create. We each commit to meeting these needs so that we can pursue our personal goals with confidence and support. Tandem riders are more productive when they know that their partner is committed to completing the marathon and, therefore, is willing to stay the course despite unexpected changes. It is no different in marriage. Spouses must be each other's number one fan if the marriage is going to have a fighting chance at accomplishing its goals. Below are some of the different ways spouses approach situations. Understanding them opens the door to the kind of adjustments we must make in support of our spouses.

Too Tired to Talk—After-Work Communication

Most men talk less—quite a bit less—at the end of the day. Women, on the other hand, view getting back together with their husbands at the end of the day as a chance to catch up and strengthen their marriages. The more a woman knows about her husband's day and the more he knows about her day, the closer she believes they will be as a couple. Since she "knows" he wants closeness too, she assumes he wants it through more communication at a time when, in actuality, he is pretty much verbally exhausted. Many men do not do well in extensive conversations at the day's end, especially if they have a job that requires verbal exchange throughout the day.

A Little Peace and Quiet—The After-Work Effort

If a guy is too tired to talk, he might well choose to spend his evening working in the garage, reading in the study, or walking by the lake. He might even collapse in front of the television: the tube is something he doesn't need to interact with. His wife, however, would like to do something with her husband or family since they have not been together all day. The potential for conflict is fairly high if we fail to learn each other's needs; to conserve our physical, mental, and emotional energy; and to balance our activities and desires around each other.

Learn what each other's energy levels are at the end of the day and be sensitive to them. Maybe each of you needs a thirty minute break before or after dinner to nap, just have some peace and quiet, or do something unrelated to what you do during the day. Whatever you do individually after the work day, be sure to come together to share something about your day with one another. It's easy to get into separate routines that eventually replace couple interaction. It may help to plan activities rather than expect spontaneously to come up with mutually acceptable activities. Planning obviously provides discussion time; it also gives each partner the opportunity to prepare physically and emotionally.

Who's on First—Sporting Events

For most men, sporting events are exciting. Their competitive nature causes many men to be avid supporters of both their teams and often many other teams as well. Since competitiveness is not as high in most women, they are usually less interested in sports, though they might find something of interest in a player's personal life. Even in women's sports, where competitive women work hard to win, there still remains an atmosphere that is very conducive to relationship building. Many men show less sensitivity to an injury that occurs in a sporting event; it is a part of the risk that accompanies the thrill of competition. In the heat of battle, whether they are participating in the event or watching it, men too often lose sight of the fact that a sport is just a game.

Men place a lower priority on the people who play the game than on the game itself; men often lack the sensitivity that is innate to women. Men get too frustrated when their team isn't doing well. Sometimes this competitive disappointment can rear its ugly head when a wife doesn't "attack" an issue with fervor or takes too long to solve a personal, relational, or professional problem. Competitive women should consider the inappropriateness of this "spirit of aggression" as well.

As team members in the marriage marathon, we are working with each other for the welfare of the marriage; we are competing against no one! Marriage is a journey upon which thousands upon thousands of couples around the world embark. Wouldn't it be great if each of us adopted the desire to see everybody win? Competition is acceptable and healthy outside of relationships, but it tends to be divisive and has little or no value within them. Marriage is a relationship, not a sport.

In the Mood for Love—Sex

For most women "love" is spelled with four letters; for most men it's spelled with three. For men, it's anytime, anywhere; window shades up or down; lights on or off. Atmosphere is only a trapping for the big moment. In the room means in the mood! For women, atmosphere is part of the entire experience. Sexual intimacy is the culmination of a great day with a man who respects what she thinks and feels. Though men will always see the highlight of sexual intimacy as "the act," they must respect the part of lovemaking that makes it pleasurable for their wives. Toby Keith's country song is pure male: "A little less talk, and a little more action." The talk may mean little to the husband, but it is important to the wife; in fact, it is the caring associated with talk that makes the relationship meaningful and lasting and intercourse more exciting. Our society has failed us in its mostly masculine portrayal of sex as the measure of romance. Sex doesn't make a romance; communication that stems from mutual respect and love does. Sex should be a product of love, not its definition.

Now What?—Questions

Men tend to view questions as meddling and bothersome, especially at the end of the day. Women, on the other hand, see them as channels through which they gain critical insight into the heart and soul of the men to whom they are willing to give everything. Here is an area where men need to adjust the way they think. Questions at work or at home should never be considered meddling unless we are dowsed in selfishness and have no concern for the growth of others. Men often feel that they have to be strong and always have the right answer; to admit otherwise is a weakness that seems too difficult to reveal. Men never accomplish good results with this attitude because it gradually isolates them from the one person who, at the outset of the marriage, wants nothing more than to help. Because men tend to have this "fewer questions" approach, we encourage wives not to try to force too much from their husbands too fast. Take it slow; men who truly care about their wives' needs will gradually open up.

Here We Go—Geographical Moves

Because women are tied more to their environment through relationships with friends and neighbors, geographical moves can be a tremendously trying time. When a move occurs, who the wife is and what is meaningful to her is being torn away, and she may truly feel threatened by the potential loss. She needs time to say good-bye to friends and to pull up roots in the community and at work. Leaving is a commitment to the man she loves who, she hopes, will understand her grief and give her time to adjust both to leaving the old community and to joining the new community. When a moving company comes in to pack the household goods, they are packing away her home, her life, and her identity. The husband should make sure they treat the furniture, knickknacks, dishes, photographs, and such things with great care. They are handling her life!

Men tend to see a move as an opportunity to achieve greater things in a new and exciting place. A man cares about the people he will leave behind, but since his identity is not tied up in these relationships, it is much easier for him to leave. He can always call them after arriving at the new location to see how they're doing. New friends and associates will come to replace the others. However, the more relational a man is or becomes, the more difficult moves are for him as well.

On the Road Again—Travel and Vacations

How does a man generally get to his next location or to his favorite vacation spot? Usually as quickly as he can and without asking for directions. Many men are convinced that the interstate is filled with people trying to beat them to wherever they want to go. Gary once had, and might still have, the speed record from Kokomo, Indiana, to Atlanta, Georgia: somewhere between thirteen and fourteen hours with a ten-month-old infant crying her eyes out the entire last hour of the trip. He'll never forget the silence and stinging stares he received from his wife as his reward. She probably thought he was possessed. It was years before he realized there were things to look at on the way to places and that the red car was not really racing him to the next town. His wife's desire to stop from time to time is now honored regularly, and he's discovered that the entire family enjoys driving a little bit more. He has even learned to stop at a gas station and not rush everyone along to get back into the race, that is the road. Life is more meaningful when we pay more attention to both the people who offer us direction and assistance on our journey as well as the places that give the journey its music and color. Take a look around you from time to time and you'll never be alone.

"9 to 5" or Dawn to Dusk—Work

Because women tend to be less competitive, their work is often of higher quality than men's. Men are so mission or goal oriented that employers need to be careful not to make an important task a competitive issue. Men can become so focused on getting to the goal that quality is sacrificed.[1] When Gary was in graduate school, he worked at an orthopedic company that made bone implants. The ability and productivity of a polisher was determined by the number of parts completed every hour. You can imagine what happened to quality from time to time. If the company hadn't had someone supervising the work, world output records for every part might have been achieved, but at what cost? Thank goodness for quality control; without it, many men would be replaced by women who would continue along at a steady pace until the work is done right.

It is unfortunate that women feel the pressure to be more like men in our society or that men pressure women to take on masculine qualities. Their conscientious style of life probably has something to do with their longer life span. It is good that men are competitive; it makes us great protectors and advocates for issues that must be handled directly. It also helps us to be more confrontational, but not everything about competitiveness is good. The sexes can learn from each other without trying to clone each other.

Looking in the Mirror—Self-Worth

Men tend to find their greatest worth in being well-respected for their effort, that is, what they do and how hard they do it. On the other hand, women tend to find their worth in the relationships they build with the people for whom they care. The one thing that a woman should not be without for any extended period of time is mutual affection.[2] Men and women see different self-images when they look in the mirror of significance.

"Just Do It"—Solving Issues

Being more solution oriented, men want to solve problems immediately, while women want to see the "big picture" before they make a decision.[3] Men want the concern or issue settled now; women tend to want to settle it after some thought and joint consideration. We need to be sensitive to these differences. When time allows, a husband should take his wife's style and slow down. They will reach a joint decision that is more beneficial, and the wife will begin to know that her husband has confidence in her. When decisions must be made quickly, a woman might do well to let her husband make the decision, or she might at least take less time to provide input. Her husband will appreciate the confidence she has put in him to make the best decision. And remember: whatever the outcome, own it together!

A Special Focus

Though there are many differences and needs that you must discover about your spouse, there is one specific area for each spouse to which special attention should be paid. Focusing on these needs works as a jump start to the Needs Cycle. The husband must always remember to validate his wife's thoughts and feelings. These two elements (thoughts and feelings) lie at the heart of who she is. On the other hand, a wife must remember that she can do great damage to her husband by failing to recognize the effort he puts forth at his job and at home. Men need praise, especially when they make improvements in how they relate to others! Meeting these two areas of need will go a long way in keeping the Needs Cycle functioning.

Summary and Strategy Progression

"I will place my spouse's needs before my own." To accept this statement is to accept a responsibility that demands we pay close attention to the thoughts, emotions, and desires of our spouses. It implies that we place our spouses on a pedestal and be their number one fans,

that we support them above all others. It is spouse-centered living rather than self-centered living.

But what does it take to maintain such a responsibility throughout the marriage marathon? Knowing who is peddling along with us is just the first phase of the strategy for maintaining a strong and productive union. There are certain key ingredients that must be part of our daily experience. These ingredients, when practiced, provide the impetus to regularly place the needs of our spouses before our own. Without these ingredients, the knowledge gained in this section will gradually fade out of memory and have no lasting effect. With these ingredients, a marriage can grow and will certainly endure.

"I will place my spouse's needs before my own."

You have just passed Marriage Marathon Milestone 1. Keep peddling!

🌿 Strategy Two 🌿

*I will daily love, honor,
and encourage my spouse.*

Commitment: Recognizing the Essential Ingredients

Caring about or wanting to meet the needs of another person does not occur in a vacuum; there is a driving factor behind good behavior. What are those basic ingredients that ensure that the commitments we make to our spouses will remain strong? And how can we be sure that our spouses will remain faithful to their commitments? We've discussed the importance of attitude and commitment for revealing the quality and quantity of our love. Attitude, commitment, and untested love function as starting blocks for the marriage marathon. But what ingredients make up the surface on which the lifelong marathon is run? There are three—love, honor, and encouragement.

At the beginning of a couple's journey together there is little doubt that they care for one another; they have made commitments to meet each other's needs. But while this untested love is not able to stand up against the trials of a grueling marathon, it is the seed from which can grow a love that replicates the heart of God and stands true to commitments that guarantee endurance and victory. Love is the foundation for constructing a surface that is able to sustain a successful marathon. Therefore, the development of untested love into unconditional love is not optional. We must understand and incorporate true love into our hearts and daily activities before our attitudes and commitments will deepen. And as our attitudes and commitments deepen, our ability to honor and encourage (the second and third essential ingredients) grow and make the surface on which we ride the marathon even stronger.

A Christian's relationship with God develops much the same way. Through His Spirit, we become aware of His presence and desire to love us. When we respond to Him, we come knowing about our imperfection yet, from a human standpoint, we possess an untested love that draws us into the relationship. Our hearts are grateful for forgiveness and salvation, and we commit to following Him, not really knowing the difficulties of the journey before us. Is this initial love that we have enough to sustain us? Hardly! Our newfound relationship with the Lord can go in at least four directions, three of which lead to disaster. The direction a life takes is dependent upon the decisions made with regard to knowing and understanding God and His word.

Some new believers hear the Word but take no time to understand how it should affect their lives; it soon becomes evident how shallow their untested love actually is as others witness these folks rejecting the Savior who loved them.

Others who are young in their faith hear the Word of God and rejoice over the blessings and promises that they have received, but as soon as difficulties and disappointments come their way, their commitments wane and the love they claimed to have had for the Lord is denied. The Lord didn't take care of them the way they expected He would; possibly they came into the relationship with the wrong motives.

Still other new Christians listen to the Word of God, but find it difficult to trust this new union for all their needs; their concerns about day-to-day life and financial security preoccupy their time so much that they have no time remaining to develop their relationship with the Lord.

Finally, there are those who hear the Word of God and understand the value of the message they received and the Person who sought them and drew them to Him. They understand the purpose of the relationship so well that they are willing to continue despite the difficulties that may develop along the way. Their knowledge and understanding of God and the ultimate purpose for the relationship strengthens their commitment to protect the relationship. The quality of their love, which was once selfish and based more on emotion than commitment, is bolstered by greater knowledge of the One who loves them, is tested by affliction, and is evidenced by service (Matt. 13:18–23). Their untested love has become unconditional; they will be with Him to the finish line!

Similarly untested or immature love in marriage is not enough to sustain the new union. Some of us marry but take little time to get to know and understand the needs and the dreams of our partner. We have married for selfish reasons and personal gain, so our marriages are immediately in distress.

Others of us spend the early days and years of our marriage getting to know one another and enjoying the fruits of married life, but as soon as one or both of us begin to experience a detour from our original plans and expectations, our commitment to the relationship dissipates and our marriages shatter upon the rocks that lie just beneath our shallow love.

Still others of us marry, establish homes, and set out to stay together for life, but eventually the pressures of daily life, our personal differences, and our desires for financial security or independence preoccupy our minds so much that the relationship is ignored until it resembles the wreck of a runaway train. The love we thought we had for one another was greater for other things than it was for our spouses.

Finally, there are those of us who appreciate the relationships we've begun and the potential they hold to give the marriage priority in our lives. We appreciate the fact that our spouses chose us as partners with whom to experience life on our journeys of unknown joys and sorrows. We adapt to and compliment each other's differences, incorporate one another's dreams into our own, and serve one another by understanding and meeting needs. Difficulties become a challenge to grow in our love for one another rather than evidence of incompatibility. An immature love that brought us together has grown into an unconditional love that will never let us part.

The essential ingredients to any relationship are *love* that endures through time, *honor* that shows value through service, and *encouragement* that guarantees hope through personal growth. Honor and encouragement are products of a maturing love. When applied daily, they form the surface on which the marriage marathon is safely completed.

Marriage Strategy 2

The importance of these three ingredients to a successful journey requires that a strategy statement be made to keep them foremost in our minds. *"I will daily love, honor, and encourage my spouse."* It is through this commitment that you are able to place your partner's needs ahead of your own and fulfill all the other strategies that are to follow. Without this commitment, the remaining strategies are no more than an academic exercise—an endeavor that leads nowhere and has little or no lasting value.

CHAPTER 5

The Many Faces of Love

To care about anyone, there must be some type of love present. But love is such a difficult concept to understand because we refer to it in so many ways. It can refer to an intense feeling for a person or a strong desire for a piece of pie. Love is associated with the emotions which make it an unstable force that tends to come and go. To understand it as a benevolent choice that functions outside the realm of emotion is generally not a part of the picture. With all the attempts to define and describe love throughout history, the confusion is understandable.

"Love Is . . ."

Journalist H. L. Mencken once described love as "being in a state of natural hysteria or being in a perpetual state of anesthesia." The movie *Love Story* introduced the concept of love being the force behind "never having to say you're sorry." There's some truth to the statement that love is "a find, a fire, a heaven, a hell where pleasure, pain, and sad repentance dwell." The bachelor Plato must have been badly stung by an offering of young love that was rejected or betrayed, for he said love was "a grave mental disease." Others offer a limited understanding of love by describing it as a "feeling you feel when you feel that you're going to get a feeling you've never felt before." The opposite of the *Love Story* corruption of the term is found in a statement of love that describes two of its characteristics: love is "an act of endless forgiveness, a tender look."

Most of these descriptions of love are either wrong or incomplete. Love may never be defined in a way that is acceptable to everybody because, in its broader sense, it involves both emotion and volition, both unselfish as well as—unfortunately—selfish acts. However, it can be described and properly understood if we more narrowly define the term to eliminate the "impurities" that confuse and cover its true meaning.

Classical Greek has given us at least four words that describe love: *stergo, erao, phileo,* and *agapao.* The first word, *stergo,* appears to be a catch-all word for love. It is an affectionate love that refers to the mutual love of parents and children, the love of a people for a ruler, as well as the love a dog can have for its master.[1] Because the word is seldom used with reference to husbands and wives, connecting it to the idea of "belonging, dependability, and security" within marriage seems to be stretching its meaning. Also, saying that *epithymia* is a Greek word for love does not appear to be supported.[2] Its meaning, which speaks of "desire, lust, passion, and longing," seems to be adequately covered by the classical Greek word, *erao.*

For these reasons, this section will introduce the three primary words for love as they are understood in classical and New Testament Greek. Special emphasis is placed on the New Testament usage of the word *agapao,* which is different from the Hellenistic understanding that primarily used it synonymously with both *erao* and *phileo,* although it slightly suggests the New Testament usage at times when used to speak of "a generous move by one for the sake of the other."[3] The New Testament word *agapao* refers not just to feelings but to actions that are taken for the welfare of others that stem from a deliberate choice. From this understanding of love logically flows the second and third essential ingredients for completing a successful marathon: honor and encouragement. They are both action words that find their source in love *(agape)*. Personal gain or selfish ambition is foreign to these ingredients.

In this section we'll describe love in its entirety so that the values of honor and encouragement can be seen as inseparably linked to it. They are the natural products of a heart that accepts the thrill and responsibilities of love.

The Making of Love

Have you ever had the misfortune of sitting in a courtroom as two lawyers pit one spouse against another in hopes of swaying a neutral judge to their client's advantage? Two individuals who had once held each other's hopes in their hands, intimately given themselves to one another, and trusted each other with secrets they would share with no one else, stand before a judge who must decide on matters, once private, now made public. Their commitment to love until parted by death has become a commitment to part before death robs them of their fair share. The immature love of one or both partners remains selfish, locked in painful emotions created by insensitive words and irresponsible acts. Their love was tested by the early stages of the marriage marathon and found lacking. Unwilling to make the necessary adjustments to continue on the journey, they disqualified themselves, and the sound of an impartial and uninvested gavel marks the end of their partnership. They misunderstood the quality and quantity of their love.

By understanding the three types of love, we are better able to develop each type of love and know which of the types deepens the others. It is everyone's responsibility to make the extension or expression of love for their spouses better. The "making of love" moves from the sensual to the volitional, ensuring that the right behavior, attitude, and action is always done for the benefit and welfare of one's spouse despite emotion and personal aspirations.

Sensual Love

Erao or *eros* describes a love that is of the senses. It's the physical appearance of another person that makes us gaze, the walk that intrigues, the smell that excites, the sound of a voice that is pleasing. This type of love is seen by our longings, cravings, and even lusts. This love is so powerful and enticing that it often defies "reason, will, and discretion on the way to ecstasy."[4] Romance is part of this kind of love. Within the confines of morality and devotion, this is a beautiful expression of openness to and caring for another person. Outside of morality, it appears in the form of stalking, sexual aggression, and selfish passion and gratification.

Eros is of the senses, physical in nature, and face to face. It can be expressed in its less passionate form as a surprise, love note, a telephone call to say I love you, or a smile across the room. More passionately it may involve wearing an exotic smelling perfume, a stunning outfit, or the playful expression of a tantalizing wink. Ultimately it embraces the sexual union that consummates the devotion a man and a woman feel for each other. Although sexual intercourse is wonderful and a necessary part of a stable marriage, it cannot be seen as "the oil in the machinery of a marriage," as some have suggested.[5] It is not the main ingredient to keeping a marriage going. Sensual love, without its cousins *phileo* and *agapao,* has a short life span because it turns the act of foreplay and lovemaking into an unpleasant duty to protect fidelity. That effort frequently fails. *Eros* is important to marriage and is great fun, but it cannot act alone.

Affectionate Love

Affectionate love refers to the closeness and fondness that people experience with others due to an attraction that may or may not be connected to *eros.* The attraction may come from common interests and goals and similar likes and dislikes. It is standing beside the person you care about to offer a shoulder or an open mind. It involves sharing, which promotes togetherness and comfort. *Phileo* refers to the warmth that a father has for his son or a spouse toward his or her partner. It does not necessarily imply a love that requires service, though it may invoke a desire to help. It is a feeling, like *eros*, but it is less passionate. It is of the heart, based on commonalities, and is shoulder to shoulder.

This type of love is expressed frequently by couples in their common appreciation for activities and things. It happens when people spend time together doing things they both enjoy and that helps them relax. This love takes couples beyond the temporary gratification of sensual love to a love that caresses and cares for the relationship and develops a closer friendship. In marriage, *phileo* makes sensual love a reward rather than a responsibility.

Volitional Love

Volitional love governs the quality and protects the motives of sensual and affectionate love. "This is not the love of complacency, or affection, that is, it is not drawn out by any excellency in its objects." *Agape* love "is not an impulse from the feelings, it does not always run with the natural inclinations, nor does it spend itself only upon those for whom some affinity is discovered. Love seeks the welfare of all"[6] apart from an emotion that may tempt one to do otherwise. It is a choice that determines to do what is right by another simply because it wants to. It is of the will, is unconditional, sacrificing personal comfort for the benefit of another, and is thoroughly selfless. In a phrase, *agape* love is *an unconditional commitment to care for the welfare of an imperfect person.*

What is remarkable about this love is that it generally provokes a loving response from those who receive it, especially in marriage, because both individuals desire to be loved by the other. However, the giving of this love is not dependent upon a response.

Dan was a hard-working man, committed both to his faith in God and to his wife, Carrie, who grew up with a father who was not very affectionate. This lack of *phileo* love eventually appeared in Dan and Carrie's marriage as Carrie found it difficult to show interest in Dan's career and activities. Because they shared few common interests, the sensual aspect of their relationship reduced itself to obligation rather than mutual enjoyment. Though emotionally hurt and sexually frustrated, Dan continued to court and pursue his wife. He accepted his wife's struggle with intimacy and committed himself to finding ways to build a friendship through newly created interests that both could share. Recently Carrie expressed an interest in camping, to Dan's disbelief. There's a good chance the camping scene will stimulate a common interest and affection between them, which may fill some of the potholes that have made their journey a little bumpy.

In a society that places its hope for marital victory in the bedroom, Dan's persistence to pursue his wife seems ill advised. But Dan's love goes beyond sensual satisfaction and common affection to an unconditional commitment from one imperfect person to another. His love looks to the welfare of his spouse before his own. He is willing to change his own interests if doing so will improve the quality of his wife's life. His love looks for common ground on which the sensual fulfillment of his marriage can flourish and mature. Though Carrie responds to Dan's attempts to create common ground, she still finds it difficult to be fully open with Dan and accepting of his shortcomings; however, Dan's love is not dependent on a proper response from Carrie. Dan and Carrie may not be traversing the marathon course as fast as others, but they are moving in the right direction.

Too often we forget the inadequate way we treat God, who loves us unconditionally. He decided to have a relationship with us and nothing can separate us (Rom. 8:31–39), not even our own tendency to get off course. He stays with us even though we hurt and grieve Him. People who are injured need someone to stay alongside them when the going is tough if they are to have any hope of recovery. God knows that His presence is essential to the healing of anyone injured by the consequences of a sinful nature; His unconditional love makes Him complete His marathon with each of us. Are we, as spouses, becoming more like Jesus Christ so that our presence in the lives of others will create good and not harm? Like Dan, do we believe that our works of love are carried out to help our spouses grow spiritually, personally, and relationally? Where love abides, relational growth is possible; where love hides, relational death is inevitable. Pursue love (1 Cor. 14:1)!

A Synopsis of Love

Sensual and affectionate love can become selfish. A man might be attracted to a woman because she has beautiful eyes and slender legs, and enjoys flying and hiking. Or a woman might be attracted to a man because he has beautiful hair and an excellent physique, and enjoys the same intellectual pursuits as she. These reasons for attraction are not necessarily wrong, in fact—they are essential to *beginning* a courtship and *enjoying* the marriage marathon—but they are personal to the individual who is making the assessment. *Agape* love is the influence that keeps the other two types of love in perspective.

When jobs are lost, feelings can change under the pressure; when children come, figures tend to shift and hobbies sometimes need to be adjusted; and with advancing age, beauty and good looks deteriorate. What keeps the selfish motives for falling in love from letting us fall out of love? What prevents shifts in feelings from making us look elsewhere for someone else who can bring "greater" pleasure? What makes a person work through difficult times, which are inevitable in marriage, to rekindle lost attraction? The answer lies in a choice that honors commitments, in a love that sacrifices its own welfare for the welfare of another. It's the kind of love that leads a wife to help her husband in the yard when he's extremely crimped for time to complete a book. *Agape* love is the commitment to build a marriage relationship whether the skies are blue or gray, whether in harvest or famine, whether in peace or war.

CHAPTER 6

Making Marriage's
Honor Roll

*J*ust as a marathon winner receives a victor's wreath or a gold medallion, so also there are spiritual rewards for successfully completing the marriage marathon. Though security, stability, peace, and contentment are welcome corollaries of working as a team throughout the marriage marathon, the crown of righteousness that the Lord will place upon our heads is second to none in value as a reward for loving one another without condition, for finishing the race with honor, and for having remained true to our commitments to one another and God (2 Tim. 4:6–8). Looking into His sanguine eyes and seeing the tranquil smile on His face as He greets and awards our striving to reflect His love to a fallen world will bring us rest in the truest sense of the word.

In the earthly sense, to make an honor roll you have to complete a task in an honorable fashion. In academic settings, honor is attained by achieving a certain grade point average throughout a degree program; in business, honor is received by meeting company goals while bringing a project to a successful closure; in sports, one is honored by being chosen to play in an all-star game because of superior play over the first half of a season or throughout a career. In the marriage marathon, a couple's lifelong commitment to one another is honored after death when a life faithful to Christ and one's spouse is awarded an imperishable crown (1 Cor. 9:24–27).

Note that in these examples, only one demands that the rewarded person possess honor as a character trait. Graduates of degree programs, business people who accomplish great projects, and athletes who amaze crowds with their talents are not required to *live honorable lives* in order to receive praise or honor. But marriage is quite different! Even in a non-Christian marriage, the character of each spouse is critical if the temporary awards of riding in a successful marathon—faithfulness, peace, and the presence of a loving spouse throughout the aging process—are to be achieved. Remember, love, honor, and encouragement form the surface on which the marriage marathon is completed. This makes character, the way one behaves and lives, critical.

Character is even more critical in a Christian marriage when the ultimate honor for riding a successful marriage marathon is received after death. In Scripture, honor as an award is inextricably linked to righteousness, loyalty, and humility. To receive honor without living honorably is as "snow in the summer and like rain in the harvest" (Prov. 26:1; 21:21; 22:4).[1] Our society is continually eliminating character from consideration when determining the value of a person's efforts. To do the same in marriage is to turn a divinely created institution designed to provide refuge, purpose, and peace into an incinerator of human hope.

In both the Old and New Testaments, figurative usages of honor, position (rank, status), character (traits), and actions that show respect or high regard for others abound and provide a thorough explanation of the concept. In its literal sense, honor carries the idea of weight and heaviness (1 Sam. 4:18, "Eli was heavy"). Figuratively it takes on the idea of value, as with wealth (Gen. 13:2), heaviness or hardness of heart (Exod. 7:14), severity of servitude (1 Kings 12:10), warfare (Judg. 20:34), and pestilence (Gen. 41:31), and the greatness and dignity associated to a position or office (Num. 22:15; Rom. 13:7; 1 Peter 2:17).

Honor usually addresses the value and worth of a person based on the position they achieved and the character with which they conducted themselves. Unique to Scripture is the idea that all people are worthy of honor because of their position of dominion in creation (Gen. 1:26–31; Ps. 8:5–8). Because God has placed intrinsic value on humanity, each individual, within the confines of justice, should be treated with respect, care, and compassion to the point of preferring another over oneself (Rom. 12:10; 1 Peter 2:17).[2]

This principle of honor is applied throughout Scripture with regard to the fair treatment of slaves (Col. 4:1), the attitude a child should have for his or her parents (Eph. 6:2), the proper care for one's wife (1 Peter 3:7), the manner in which spouses conduct sexual intimacy (1 Thess.

4:4–5), and the respect shown to widows, elders, and responsible leaders in the church (1 Tim 5:3; 5:17; Phil. 2:29).[3] In order to maintain unity in the church, Paul admonished the Corinthians to remember that "God has so composed the body, giving more abundant honor to that member which lacked, that there should be no division in the body, but that *the members should have the same care for one another*" (1 Cor. 12:24–25 NASB, emphasis added). Honor implies care!

For example, honorable people of power care for their subjects; honorable teachers would never deceive their students; honorable clerks would never steal from their employers; an honorable wife would never invalidate her husband's thoughts; and an honorable husband would not think of leaving his wife for any reason. At a minimum, honor places the needs of others equal to one's own, but often it places them before one's own. It shouts for the worth of one individual to be established by the thoughtful consideration and tactful care of another individual. In marriage, it suggests that we place our spouses in a position higher than us, on a pedestal of praise. Without care or intentional acts of kindness, our spouses are devalued and honor is dissolved.

The Making of Honor

We don't attain honor easily. It is the product of our upbringing, the result of established values and understanding that have been developed throughout our life. It is a trait inextricably bound and dependent upon the amount of love, wisdom, and care that we have experienced from others. Honor is a learned trait. We cannot be honorable simply because we have attained a position of honor or desire to be honorable. Honor is the gift of wisdom that comes from sound instruction (Prov. 4:1–9).

If we have been taught to look out for the concerns of number one or to do whatever is best for ourselves as long as others are not affected negatively, there is little chance, if any, that honor will develop as a natural trait in our lives and decision-making capabilities. If we are led to believe that others are responsible for our happiness or if we are warned that we can trust no one but ourselves, honor will not develop. As long as we view other people as a threat or as a tool, the development of honor is halted.

Honor is developed from ideas that affirm the basic value of other people's worth, their right to pursue peace, succeed, know the truth, and be treated fairly. Without these underlying assumptions, people will live dishonorably by stepping on others in pursuit of personal achievement, avoiding accountability for their actions, using positions of authority to control and abuse others, all with no remorse for the lying, cheating, and stealing that accompany such actions.

Honor does not exist where there is conflict for personal gain, secret agendas, or an attitude of superiority. Rather, it flows from the heart of a person who understands the innate and priceless worth of others and seeks to employ personal skills and insights for the betterment of others. Honor upholds the truth, even when the truth produces no personal benefit. Honor exists where there is a genuine concern that others have an equal chance to reach their fullest potential. "I cannot lie, cheat, or steal because I love God and those He created. He deserves my loyalty and they deserve my respect." Love for others demands that we honor them as well.

Honor is bestowed or developed. As we travel along in our marriages, we must overcome philosophies, past experiences, and our own natural human tendencies that entice us to put ourselves before our spouses. We must recognize our partners' innate, God-given worth and live in a manner that protects and perpetuates it.

The Place of Honor

Honor is completely dependent on love, the first essential ingredient we discussed. Without love, it is impossible to honor. Things that we honor, we cherish and keep in good working order. Things we dishonor are treated lightly, and if they dissipate like the mist from a spray bottle, nothing is lost. Honor is a decision we make—sometimes by the minute or by the hour, but mostly on a daily basis—to place value upon an object or person; it results in loving actions toward the object or person we honor. Honor is love applied! Every action that we do for the benefit of our spouses is an act of honor. To spend time together, hear a story from the day's events, love our children, clean the garage, prepare a meal, help each other in the yard, attend an event that is special only to our spouses, refrain from speaking a harsh word, or make a special call during a busy day when we're away from home are all acts that honor our spouses. They remind our spouses that their worth is immeasurable in our eyes.

Priorities often betray our loyalties. That to which we give the most time is what we honor and love. It doesn't take our spouses long to see where we place our heart. Sometimes it is healthy for us to pause and evaluate the time we spend with and for our spouses and families against the time we spend doing things that are more individual in nature. Often we fall into routines that do not help create stability in our marriages. There is nothing inherently wrong with being financially frugal, having friends of the opposite gender, enjoying the outdoors by hiking, doing lawn care, hunting, or trap-shooting, occasionally bringing home work from the office or taking an extra job, developing a hobby, or playing in intramural sports programs *unless* these activities take priority over time spent with our spouses. If our spouses believe that our outside friendships or activities are more important to us than our marriages, adjustments *must* be made. An occasional honor checkup is never out of order. All we need to do is spot the weakness and make the adjustment that shows that love is the motivating force in our relationships.

Respect: A Natural Corollary to Honor

One of the best ways we can honor our spouses is through respect. In marriage, respect involves looking back to see our spouses' accomplishments and then appropriately responding to those accomplishments in direct proportion to their value. The difficulty with marriage is that we get so busy fulfilling our respective roles that we never stop to fully gain an appreciation for all the things our spouses are doing to keep the marriage marathon on course. We need to pause and *look back* over the past weeks and months to discover how valuable the other member of the team is to our marriages. Please look at the sample worksheets (pp. 86–87). Note your spouse's activities over the past week or month. After you have filled out the sheet, give it to your spouse to fill in any activities that you may have missed. After you both have completed this phase of the respect check, take the second sheet and identify five activities that you most appreciate in your spouse.

Once you have identified at least five of your spouse's activities, try to do something special that tangibly shows your appreciation of his or her efforts. A thank you is great, but try harder: a card, a kiss, a dinner out, changing roles for a day. Each act of appreciation, as well as a well-deserved thank you, is an expression of respect. They show that you are willing to take time from your busy schedule to remember the valuable efforts of the spouse who loves you and wants to be loved. Your appreciation, in word and deed, assures your spouse that you take seriously the most important human relationship you have. Respect is an intentional act that rewards the many responsibilities each spouse must

WORKSHEET I
RESPECT CHECK

WEEKDAYS		WEEKENDS	
0600		0600	
0630		0630	
0700		0700	
0730		0730	
0800		0800	
0830		0830	
0900		0900	
0930		0930	
1000		1000	
1030		1030	
1100		1100	
1130		1130	
1200		1200	
1230		1230	
100		100	
130		130	
200		200	
230		230	
300		300	
330		330	
400		400	
430		430	
500		500	
530		530	
600		600	
630		630	
700		700	
730		730	
800		800	
830		830	
900		900	
930		930	
1000		1000	

Please note your spouse's activities over the past week to one month!

take on to maintain a growing relationship. Never assume that your relationship is so secure that it no longer needs regular expressions of respect or appreciation. There is nothing better than having a partner cheering you on throughout the climbs and rapid descents of a winding marriage marathon.

WORKSHEET II
RESPECT CHECK

I respect _____ because he/she:

1. _____

2. _____

3. _____

4. _____

5. _____

Track your spouse's incredible deeds!

CHAPTER 7

Encouragement: Turning Possibility into Progress

*W*e begin the marriage marathon with dozens of possibilities that excite and motivate us. Love has driven us to choose teammates, and our belief in each other's worth confirms our conviction that together we are capable of accomplishing good things. But what completes the picture? What turns possibility into progress? What makes the course we travel less complex and more congenial?

Encouragement Happens . . .

- when you call your spouse at work just to say "I love you."
- when you say "You're right about . . ."
- when you praise your spouse publicly.
- when you don't remind your spouse of past mistakes.
- when you allow your spouse to pursue his or her love of sailing, even though you have no interest in the activity at all.
- when you recognize your spouse's lack of interest in your hobby and shorten your participation in it.
- when you say thank you for the smallest effort your spouse makes to put you first.
- when you let your spouse find a solution to a problem he or she shares with you.
- when you help your spouse accomplish something that he or she had never thought possible.
- when you gently place your arm around your spouse after he or she has spoken harshly to you.
- when you don't push away your spouse's attempts at peace.

- when you don't compare your spouse's inabilities with the abilities of others.
- when you keep your eyes and heart focused on the loveliness of your aging spouse.
- when you understand that the roles each spouse plays do not require perfection.
- when you invite and honor your spouse's opinions in the decision-making process.
- when you take the time to be thoughtful and intentional in your actions toward your spouse.

It happens only when you make it happen!

The Making of Encouragement

Encouragement ensures that our spouses are going to remain capable of completing the marathon. It guarantees that our partners will be physically, intellectually, emotionally, morally, and spiritually able to both withstand and enjoy the experiences of living together. And should they falter along the way, encouragement allows for restoration. Encouragement accepts what is imperfect and reinforces the commitment to preparing and shaping weakness into strength. Encouragement is the indispensable quality and the final ingredient for the surface on which the marriage marathon is raced, making it smooth for safe and lasting travel.[1]

Love drives us to know and understand our spouses, honor forces us to deal fairly with our spouses, and encouragement compels us to selflessly care for our spouses. Encouragement is the ultimate expression of love; it takes what is weak and makes it strong, it takes what is good and makes it better, it takes potential and makes it reality, it takes problems and finds solutions, it takes disappointment and turns it into hope.

This third ingredient is completely dependent upon the first and second ingredients, for without love and honor, it is impossible to give encouragement. Encouragement takes honor and respect to another level. It doesn't assist personal growth through appreciation, it creates personal growth. Encouragement is more than noticing our partners' daily activities. It is a proactive concern that helps them reach as many of their goals and potentials as possible. Encouragement means to impart strength and confidence. When we encourage our spouses, we inspire them with hope, courage, and confidence; we support and stimulate them. It is the quality we practice as we help our spouses reach their fullest potential.

To love and honor our spouses results naturally in encouragement. Who does not want to be an encourager for someone they are devoted to and who is devoted to them? Encouragement is helping our partners prepare for a test or finish a project, supporting our spouses' desire for further education, listening to their struggles with coworkers, hearing their new ideas with excitement, expending energy for their interests, and not letting mistakes seem like the end of the world. The ultimate encouragement occurs when we help our spouses to trust in the God of the impossible. A world of possibilities is opened and realized when we daily exemplify the love of God to our spouses.

CHAPTER 8

Creating a Lasting Legacy

*I*n the spiritual life of a Christian and the church, at least three ingredients are necessary for a victorious journey through life. Christians are exhorted to love God and their neighbor (Deut. 6:5; Matt. 22:37–40; John 13:34; 1 Peter 4:8), honor God and prefer others to themselves (1 Tim. 1:17; Rev. 4:11; Rom. 11:36; 12:10), and edify or equip one another for faithful service to God and others (Eph. 4:12; Heb. 10:23–25). Through obedience to these simple concepts comes a fruitful life, Christian community, and a welcome smile from the Lord as we cross the finish line victorious over death (1 Cor. 15:54–58). And those we leave behind, both family and friends, have a legacy of faithful living and service to pass on to those who will follow them.

The accuracy of the gospel tomorrow has much to do with the accuracy with which we represent it today (Deut. 6:4–13). Carl F. H. Henry reminds us that "we are on the threshold of the decade of destiny, in the last generation before we leave behind the twentieth century, the end of one century and the beginning of another. What spiritual situation do we bequeath not only to those who follow us, but also to our contemporaries?"[1] The ingredients that comprise a solid pathway to spiritual success today and tomorrow are the same ingredients that pave the way to success in marriage and a healthy family legacy.

To Our Children's Children's Children— The Family Legacy

It doesn't take much effort to discover that the institution of marriage in America is in chaos and jeopardy. Cohabitation, homosexuality, bisexuality, premarital pleasures, and divorce characterize much of what we see, hear, and are taught through television, radio, and literature. Shervert H. Frazier believes that

> population pressures and other economic factors continue to diminish the size of the American family. Marriage is in sharp decline, cohabitation is growing, traditional families are on the endangered list, and the single-person household is the wave of the future. [S]tatistics relating to marriage, divorce, cohabitation, teen sex, out-of-wedlock births, sexually transmitted diseases (STDs), contraception, and adultery tell a tale of what has been called a "postmarital society" in continued pursuit of sexual individuality and freedom.[2]

Placing individual happiness above maintaining responsible relationships has devastated the American family. The Council on Families in America, which consists of volunteers from "interdisciplinary groups of citizens from across the human sciences and across the political spectrum," clearly describes the disaster perpetrated by the divorce revolution:

> America's divorce revolution has failed. The evidence of failure is overwhelming. The divorce revolution—by which we mean the steady displacement of a marriage culture by a culture of divorce and unwed parenthood—has created terrible hardships for children. It has generated poverty within families. It has burdened us with unsupportable social costs. It has failed to deliver on its promise of greater adult happiness and better relationships between men and women.[3]

We do not offer this assessment lightly. We recognize that these failures have been unanticipated and unintended. The divorce revolution set out to achieve some worthy social goals: to foster greater equality between men and women; to improve the family lives of women; and to expand individual happiness and choice. We recognize the enduring importance of these social goals.

Yet the divorce revolution has not brought us closer to these goals but has cast us at greater distance from them. Relationships between men and women are not getting better; by many measures, they are getting worse. They are becoming more difficult, fragile, and unhappy. Too many women are experiencing chronic economic insecurity. Too many men are isolated and estranged from their children. Too many people are lonely and unconnected. Too many children are angry, sad, and neglected.

We believe it is time to change course. The promises of the divorce revolution proved empty, its consequences devastating for both adults and children. *It is time to shift the focus of national attention from divorce to marriage.* It is time to rebuild a family culture based on enduring marital relationships.[4] (emphasis added)

The need to create a legacy based on the biblical blueprint God has established for the institution of marriage has never been greater. With the failure of the divorce revolution, a vacuum of instability, emptiness, and longing for purpose has developed. And the church is experiencing this same vacuum because of its secularization and because many who have suffered from the "divorce revolution" have come to Christ looking for answers that will provide stability to their troubled and divided families. Christian couples and teachers of the faith have a tremendous responsibility to reflect in their own lives and teachings the strategies God has provided to assist His children in creating a legacy of hope.

The late 1960s and 1970s introduced values into the American psyche that became the framework around which selflessness and committed love lost meaning. Personal peace and affluence became the focal points of human existence. Francis Schaeffer noted a quarter century ago:

Personal peace means just to be left alone, not to be troubled by the troubles of other people, whether across the world or across the city—to live one's life with minimal possibilities of being personally disturbed. Personal peace means wanting to have my personal life pattern undisturbed in my lifetime, regardless of what the result will be in the lifetimes of my children and grandchildren. Affluence means an over-whelming and ever-increasing prosperity—a life made up of things, things, and more things—a success judged by an ever higher level of material abundance.[5]

In a world that promotes personal peace or individualism as a major key to happiness, meaningful relationships have become no more than a hope. Individualism and marriage are mutually exclusive concepts. The individualist attempts to survive either without anyone or with a person who will meet the needs of the individualist. The result of this "me first" philosophy is relational frustration, loneliness, and isolation. Marriage demands selfless and sacrificial commitment on the part of both spouses. The result of this "other's first" philosophy is peace and companionship.

What happens to generations of children whose parents are busy pursuing professional and personal lives, intent on having it all, and too confident that they can leave their children under the watchful eye of the local daycare center? These children often come into the world as "mistakes" who interfere with their parents' goals. And while the parents are pursuing these goals, they often erroneously believe they can also maintain romantic and growing marriage relationships. As a result, children frequently become the victims when the cannon shells of disappointment explode around them and their parents. They become the emotional support for parents who don't have the time or inclination, or perhaps the knowledge, to maintain a healthy relationship with one another.

Some parents try to make their children their buddies rather than expend the time, energy, and commitment that rearing children demands. The unfortunate truth is that often parents are too focused on themselves to deal with the difficulty of teaching values, or they believe that children should be able to find their own way in the world. After all, the parents themselves have to be successful in their own right or at least have a life of their own. More and more children are growing up in violent homes, single-parent homes, daycare centers, and with parents who view marriage with a "hope and prayer" and something that they can easily rid themselves of if it doesn't meet their selfish expectations.

The Council on Families in America rightly concludes: "Unless we reverse the decline of marriage, no other achievements will be powerful enough to reverse the trend of declining child well-being."[6] The value of marriage lies in the hands of those who represent it to the children. The children will grow up to reflect what they have learned in the home. The institution of marriage is the foundation for a healthy society, even though about half of its players have been striking out.[7]

Cohabitation is a common choice for a generation whose parents neglected biblical marriage principles.[8] The tolerance of homosexual marriages reflects a generation's misunderstanding of what marriage actually is. Many have failed to see marriage working for the benefit of society. Instead they witnessed a legacy of failure and have decided to throw out the institution with its "outdated" ideas. The utter chaos in the American family has created a tendency to rethink the value of the institution of marriage. Who better to reestablish that value, in both the church and in the secular world, than Christians who possess the instructions for and pattern their marriages after the marriage success model provided directly from the hand of its Designer?

The care that one spouse gives to another has the same impact as a pebble cast into a still pond. Its ripple effect spreads out far beyond its initial impact. The same occurs when love, honor, and encouragement are daily given to a spouse. Loving, honoring, and encouraging one another today will be seen by our children, who will spread the message to our grandchildren. Children will be more willing to care for aging parents if they received from those parents the love they deserved as valued members of the family and of humanity. Not only will our children have the opportunity to apply our examples to their own marriages, they may also one day apply our examples to us in our later years.

Coping skills and good values are not innate. They are learned within the parameters of the family. When we focus on our spouses' needs by loving, honoring, and encouraging them daily, we give our children, friends, and associates a better opportunity to acquire this same focus (1 Cor. 7:14). The future is brighter for all who are associated with a couple who apply the unconditional volitional aspect of love to their marriage.

Here is a final thought. Because so many of our families have been separated by distance and broken marriages, children often grow up without the influence of grandparents, aunts, uncles, and family friends who espouse the same values. Parents and single parents fight the battle for their children's minds with little or no support. A family legacy must begin somewhere; let it start with you. Regardless of what your past disappointments may have been, start today to approach your marriage from a biblical perspective. Apply the strategies outlined in this book to your marriage. Work for the day that you, as a grandparent, can have the privilege of supporting your son or daughter as they raise children who love God, their spouses, family, friends, and their country.

Gary was recently reminded of this important aspect of family legacy when his mother sat down to listen to and advise his teenage daughter. When teenage children reach that phase when they are convinced that Mom and Dad just don't understand, it is refreshing to know that Nana or Pops is also there to provide a positive influence.

Summary and Strategy Progression

Love—an unconditional commitment to the welfare of an imperfect spouse—together with decisive acts of honor and encouragement set a marriage on a course that difficult challenges can never alter. These three ingredients create a potential that is limited only by a couple's imagination. The Needs Cycle is perpetually in motion and functioning with couples who together commit to living their lives with these three essential ingredients. Contentment, intimacy, stability, and satisfaction will be the experience of any couple who daily love, honor, and encourage one another. *Without love, it is impossible to give your spouse honor, and we don't encourage what we do not honor!*

We place our spouses' needs before our own by daily loving, honoring, and encouraging them. A strategy to love requires us to understand everything we can—good or bad—about our spouses so that we can better meet our spouses' personal and relational needs. We must honor our spouses as cherished friends, respect our spouses for their efforts, and encourage our spouses to achieve their goals. Although our human imperfection creates potholes along the way, a road paved with love, honor, and encouragement will limit the impact of the bumps we encounter, giving us a safer and smoother ride to the finish line.

"I will place my spouse's needs before my own."

"I will daily love, honor, and encourage my spouse."

You have just passed Marriage Marathon Milestone 2. Keep peddling!

❧ Strategy Three ❧

I will practice a style of communication that allows my spouse to be vulnerable and honest at all times.

Effective Communication: Evaluating the Health of Your Marriage

Many couples claim that their greatest concern in their marriage is the continuing lack of communication.[1] During the courting years and the first few years of marriage, communication never seemed to be a problem, but gradually they started getting comfortable or busy and began taking each other for granted. A child or two came along, social responsibilities and work became time consuming, and communication with one another deteriorated. If it is true that we only encourage what we honor and love, then it is equally true that what we don't encourage, we don't honor and love. Over time, familiarity and busyness take the focus away from our spouses and place it on other things that seem too important to ignore. Eventually our love shifts from our spouses to the things we believe *must* be taken care of to keep ahead of the bills and the neighbors. But remember, love is evidenced by what we honor and encourage.

A Marriage Indicator

There is nothing more difficult than trying to ride in a bicycle marathon when you have a high temperature, especially when you're riding the marathon in tandem. If one of the tandem is sick, both are affected. When we struggle with communication, the energy that moves our marriages forward is depleted; it's as if a fever has drained our marriages of strength. Communication is a means through which we honor and encourage our spouse, therefore communication becomes an indicator for the amount of love, honor, and encouragement taking place in our marriages.

Heat is to a thermometer what the three essential ingredients are to communication. The less frequently the essential ingredients are applied in a marriage, the less often communication occurs. It doesn't take too much absence of the essential ingredients to cause serious difficulty in communication. If a human body, whose normal temperature is 98.6 degrees, loses only 3.6 degrees of heat, it begins to shiver; if it loses just 12.6 degrees, an individual loses consciousness; if the body reaches down to a temperature of 62.6 degrees (a temperature that many would consider a comfortable outdoor climate), there is no hope of recovery. Marriages suffer the same fate when the essential ingredients begin to disappear. The degree of difficulty we have with communication is in proportion to the degree of love, honor, and encouragement in our marriages.

A Cold Front

When the essential ingredients are missing from marriage, we feel like a cold front has descended on our hopes and dreams. We may still say that we care for our spouses, but reality suggests that we are taking our marriages for granted. It's important to note that this lack of attention is generally initiated by a goal-oriented male who "captured" his wife at the altar and now is on to conquering other goals (goal-oriented, career-minded women tend to do the same thing). This may seem a bit harsh, but far too often, it's true. The warmth that once created a mutual attraction is being penetrated by a subtle coolness that could lead to a stormy relationship and cause a delay in the progress of the marriage marathon.

Although some of us intentionally shift our love away from our partners because of pride and selfish interests and attitudes, many of us simply lack the skills to adequately reflect our love in the day in and day out atmosphere of marriage. But there is hope. Communication is a skill that can be learned! Some of us have family-of-origin issues that hinder our ability to identify the concerns and needs of our spouses. In the past, these concerns may have been seen as minor details or something our spouses should be able to handle. Such neglected spouses begin to realize that they married difficult persons or they become frustrated over a lack of sensitivity. Consequently, spouses begin to pull away from each other, unable to discuss their thoughts and feelings for fear of offending or being accused of saying something that the other partner considers ridiculous or "no big deal." Because *attention to daily detail* is fading and complete trust in our partners is not a certainty, productive communication dwindles into just the necessary shop talk in order to get by. Sometimes both people sense the change; in other cases, only one of the spouses is aware of the downward spiral.

The Communication Gap

When we get married, we actually know very little about our spouses. We simply haven't known them long enough. We are shocked to find that their love is suspect and find the possibility that trust may be lacking unthinkable. It is important to remember that we came into marriage as two individuals. Frequently our backgrounds are quite different. For a lifetime, we have handled things a certain and "right" way, and we may be taken aback by our spouses' lack of understanding for proper procedure. This communication gap makes riding a tandem bicycle a little tenuous at the outset of the marathon. Many of us spend the early years of marriage trying to make our spouses into clones of ourselves so we can have peace. Rather than appreciating the differences and discovering how these differences can be joined together to uncover the uniqueness of our unions, we struggle against our spouses and slowly withdraw from developing a team approach in our journey. Unfortunately this approach simply widens the communication gap.

A natural communication gap exists at the outset of every marriage that is caused by understandable differences. If we learn to respect one another and have the skills to communicate our differences, we can bridge this gap and learn to use each other's differences for the benefit of the union, or at least appreciate and provide support for some of the struggles that our spouses' upbringings may have produced. If we don't expect perfection, and if we accept our responsibility to meet our spouses' needs and can accept the changes that come from joining two lives, the gap that would have kept us from growing closer to one another is bridged and our ability to work better in tandem is strengthened.

Mike and Stephanie came to counseling full of anger and disappointment. Stephanie was convinced that Mike wanted nothing to do with the marriage; and Mike was certain that Stephanie's overbearing spirit was the problem. On the surface, they may have been right. Because of Stephanie's anger and controlling attitude, Mike wanted little to do with the marriage.

But the actual problem went much deeper. Each spouse had personal concerns that the other either didn't know about or didn't know how to resolve. Stephanie expected Mike to understand and provide support without his having the benefit of understanding her past. Mike thought Stephanie was insensitive to his job responsibilities and demanded too much of his time. They were both overly focused on their own expectations and needs and lacked the ability to communicate their concerns openly and without threat. The space between the front and back seats of their tandem bicycle was so great that they could only hear the screams of a distraught wife or the silence of a distant husband. They definitely had a problem—lack of communication.

Marriage Strategy 3

This section is designed to present communication skills that develop trust, enhance confidence and intimacy, and enable forgiveness. It will also illustrate the different styles of communication that help and hinder the marriage marathon. True love for your spouse pursues open and honest communication. Learning communication skills helps you keep the honor and encouragement that come from love flowing toward your spouse. Good communication skills bring the seats of the tandem bicycle close enough so that turns in the road can be executed safely and the straightaways can be covered efficiently.

The inability to communicate in a spouse-centered way makes conversation unnecessarily vulnerable and openness risky. If a person cannot speak in a way that is understandable, respectful, and sincere, messages will constantly be misread and appear hurtful. Spouses must commit to a style of communication that is consistent with the previous strategy statements. Without a spouse-centered style of communication, the previous commitments appear as no more than hypocritical gestures. *How we say things validates what we say.*

Because we are naturally defensive, it is difficult for us to accept criticism and change, but both will inevitably come. It is important that we have a strategy to help us overcome the desire to resist. *"I will practice a style of communication that allows my spouse to be vulnerable and honest at all times"* regardless of how uncomfortable the issue may be to me.

CHAPTER 9

Setting a Foundation with Honesty and Vulnerability

*M*arriage needs an environment for communication that allows for vulnerability, but without risk. If you or your spouse believe that certain topics are taboo, issues will be sidestepped and growth will be hindered. If you can't handle particular subjects, you need to admit that you are too focused on your own issues and not enough on your partner's. The consequence of hidden issues is hidden needs; the consequence of hidden needs is an inability to care for each other. Vulnerability without risk is essential to healthy communication and the benefits that ensue.

Levels of Communication

Communication in marriage takes place on at least five levels.[1] As communication rises from one level to the next, vulnerability increases. The ability or inability to talk freely at each level determines the degree of closeness or isolation that we experience. As we move to each level, the content and vulnerability in the discussion intensify. *The first level is easy.* It involves sharing safe facts, explanations, and information. A work schedule, the weather, the stock market report, and daily news are discussed at this level. "What's the forecast?" "Who won the game?" "What did the market do?" Personal growth can occur at this level through the increased knowledge of facts, but relational growth is negligible.

At the second level, we share the ideas and opinions of other people. "My boss said . . ." or "Jan at work thinks . . ." Because we don't own the ideas, there is little vulnerability attached to the data. It is easy to dump responsibility for the information in the lap of someone else. Remaining at this level of communication does very little for relational growth because nothing is being revealed about our own thoughts and feelings.

We may never know each other fully because life experiences hit people in undetermined and unexpected ways. To some degree, we never know ourselves. Each of us is made up of hundreds, possibly thousands of puzzle pieces that, when joined together, present a picture of who we are. We come to a better understanding of ourselves when these pieces are gradually joined together by life's experiences and challenges. Gradually we get a fairly good picture of who we are, our strengths and weaknesses. The only way others see this picture is when we reveal ourselves in an environment that permits us to be vulnerable without risk of being belittled or criticized. If we are going to develop healthy relationships with our spouses, the next three levels of communication must be reached. The more pieces we are able to put together, the more beautiful the pictures of our lives and our lives as couples can be. Never forget that your pictures remain incomplete until the marathon is completed—life, and your marriages, are a painting in progress. However, without knowledge of the ones we love, our attempts to honor and encourage may miss their marks and needs will go unmet.

The third level involves sharing our own ideas and opinions. "I think . . ." or "I prefer. . . ." Here we take risks to see if our thoughts (subjective ideas and suggestions) will be validated or given consideration by our spouses. It's like placing a hand out to see if it will be slapped. If our spouses appear to reject us, we stop revealing personal data and revert to discussing the weather. The puzzle of who we are is kept securely inside, and we shut it away. Our spouses have lost the opportunity to interact with us on issues and to understand us. When we appear to reject our spouses, the same thing happens. The opportunity for our relationships to grow is delayed or even lost.

The fourth level of communication reveals our professional preferences, beliefs, concerns, and experiences. This level goes beyond personal opinions or suggestions, from which we may be more easily swayed, and reveals strong personal convictions. A deeper level of trust is being created as we work our relationships to this level. To discredit our spouses' experiences or personal convictions can create separation, distance, and hard feelings. Our spouses thought they could trust us, but we surprised them with a smirk or a laugh about a personal position that they gave much time, study, and reflection to reach. Our spouses recoil from the experience. Trust has been lost. Any further growth in the relationship will be difficult, if not impossible.

All relationships begin with a vulnerability that must be appreciated and protected unless we prefer to live in isolation. To have good relationships, we need to see the pieces of our spouses' puzzle from their perspective, rather than the way we want them to be. We can't appreciate and respect our partners until we know and appreciate their life experiences. Prejudice and discrimination, even of our spouses, come from ignorance, which generally comes from an unwillingness to listen to the other person's perspective. Our spouses are important, and their views are crucial to our marriages.

The final level of communication introduces us to the most vulnerable parts of our spouses' life: their emotions or inner feelings, likes, and dislikes. When our partners open up to us at this level, they believe that we love them and that sharing personal feelings with us is safe. All of us need to be open with someone; we are not naturally creatures of isolation. In marriage, there is a simple expectation that our greatest fears and joys will be accepted, or at least understood and protected, by our spouses. Nothing is more damaging to a marriage than the deterioration of trust. And trust is lost when our spouses, believing that they can be vulnerable with us and share personal views and the emotions that accompany them, are belittled, ignored, or told how wrong they are.

Our spouses need to feel safe at any level of communication so that the puzzle of their lives can be better understood. When we are unable to provide a safe environment for communication, we not only eliminate our chance to know our spouses and subsequently meet their needs, we also prevent our spouses from gaining greater insight into their lives. A neutral or hostile environment for communication keeps the important issues of our spouses in the dark and decreases our ability to love them with honor and encouragement. *Level five communication needs to become as safe as communication delivered at the first level.* When this occurs, trust grows stronger, vulnerability diminishes, and openness makes riding together in the marathon a meaningful and memorable adventure.[2]

CHAPTER 10

Building Trust
for Greater Intimacy

*T*rust is intrinsically linked to communication that is deeply personal. The more one is able to share personal thoughts and feelings about issues of the heart, the more trust is developed. This implies that trust is not often as strong as we think it is at the outset of a marriage. In the same way that we overestimate the degree of our love, we overestimate the degree of our trust. Too often we assume that love and trust in one another is a "given." Such an assumption is misleading. This is because experience has simply not been sufficient to test and validate the depth of love and trust in a marriage. Time will provide the experiences; realistic expectations will offer the hope. Love and trust grow with commitment to principles that protect them and with skills to practice them.

When a marathon team pairs up, they naturally have an innate trust in each other, but practice on the course in preparation for the race will determine whether that trust grows or fades. If either rider believes that the other is in the race for selfish reasons, that partner's willingness to take risks, to push ahead, will diminish. However, the more the two believe in each other's work ethic, know about each other's personal accomplishments and setbacks, and commit to the welfare of each other, the greater their trust, and the greater their confidence in one another. They will win together with equal praise and occasionally fail together, but with no blame.

The Trust Cycle

Everyone has some degree of innate trust simply because we are social creatures who want relationships. Only those with wounded hearts, or

...at isolation will bring peace, distance
. To develop a friendship with anyone, we
sk. As we take risks at the various levels
the vulnerability of the experience, trust
:lops. The depth of the friendship is
>mmunication. Friends begin to develop
eir trust grows.

...ps grow the same way, through a cycle of trust
that places each spouse in a journey up the levels of communication. As we reveal pieces of our puzzles to each other, trust continues to grow or spiral upward; innate trust becomes trust achieved by experience. Eventually, we develop a greater confidence and intimacy as a result of our growing trust in one another. We progress through the levels of communication, allowing each other to be *vulnerable without risk,* and therefore we reap the reward of trust, confidence, and intimacy.

There is no "Plan B" for developing trust if the "Plan A" outlined above fails. Honest communication is pursued by a heart of love that longs to piece together the puzzle of a spouse who is full of potential. With trust that is bolstered by unconditional love, each spouse helps the other adjust the pieces of his or her life to form a beautiful representation of the image of God (Eph. 5:27). Without a trust that is achieved through vulnerable and honest communication, each abandons the other to isolation. Isolation often leaves him or her open to the carnivorous appetite of the one who longs to devour the injured prey, those who are overwhelmed by the challenges of the marriage marathon (1 Peter 5:8).

A word of caution! Trust is like a huge spring. It takes a whole lot longer to wind it than it does to unwind it. Protect trust at all costs with the ingredients that make marriage the adventure of a lifetime. Love, honor, and encouragement constitute the road on which trust, confidence, and intimacy make their way.

Two Prerequisites to Effective Communication

How does a spouse unlock a wounded heart, a heart that attempted to make a critical turn on the road of personal growth, but crashed into the insensitivity or ingenuousness of a parent, friend, or employer? Many of us learn principles of communication and trust too late, and we suffer the consequences. Some of us marry individuals who have suffered from life's injustices and have chosen to keep pieces of their puzzle away from us. Knowing that hidden pieces keep a picture incomplete and that growing relationships are dependent upon knowledge of one another, we must create an environment that is conducive to openness.

Vulnerability without risk can be maintained in marriage when *both spouses accept* two statements and treat them as antidotes against a dormant disease that lurks in our hearts: self-perspectivitis. The first statement reflects a commitment to the first three strategy statements, "I care about my spouse." Attitude has much to do with the way we treat our spouses. No one subjects themselves to a struggle without caring for or believing in an issue. If we believe in and care for our spouses, we will endure the pains that accompany growth through understanding. Often assuming that we care for our spouses is self-deceiving. Sometimes our unwillingness to listen indicates an unwillingness to care. If we don't admit to such a weakness, it can never be transformed. We must actively care for our spouses if we are to help them grow.

Second, we must accept the statement that "my spouse will never lie to me." It's critical to remember that this statement is made in the context of a strategy that *strongly suggests that each spouse places the needs of the other above his or her own*. To use this statement to abuse or manipulate a spouse is impossible in this context. Speaking the truth is essential to full disclosure and understanding. If I believe that my wife lies to me, I will question many of the revealed pieces of her puzzle. As my wife senses my disbelief in her story, communication becomes too vulnerable, disclosure diminishes, and relational growth is shut down.

In our counseling experiences, we have learned that couples often assume a spouse is lying when, in fact, the opposite is the case. Once we believe that our spouses lie, the tendency to question everything is heightened. Believing our spouses lie will forever place our relationships in jeopardy. Because of this, we need to stop and evaluate four possibilities about apparent lying before we accept the idea that "my spouse is lying." Each of these possibilities may be true and an honest evaluation of them often resolves any question about lying: (1) "I can easily misunderstand my spouse"; (2) "My spouse can fail to express himself or herself clearly"; (3) "One or both of us may not have understood all the facts"; and (4) "My spouse may fear retribution" (because vulnerability without risk doesn't exist in your marriage). Though lying is wrong, it is understandable why a spouse might shade the truth when there is no safe environment in which the truth can be shared.

It's much easier to communicate when both spouses care about each other and refuse to believe that one would lie to the other. Lying is inconsistent with the strategies that give marriage the potential to be a refuge from disharmony.

CHAPTER 11

Developing Better Communication Skills

*N*ot all problems in communication revolve around a spouse's unwillingness to share thoughts, emotions, and desires. Often the problem lies in the inability to communicate—a simple lack of skills. The hope for a deeper love, the desire to honor and encourage, and a longing to trust may exist, but the lack of good communication skills makes the hills of the marriage marathon insurmountable. Desire alone is never a substitute for good skills, but it can help us pursue them.[1]

"What I Meant to Say Was . . ."—Explaining Skills

In order for a message to be understood by the recipient, the sender must first understand the message. For this to be done, communication specialists have identified six zones through which people deliver clear messages to themselves and others. Initially, a *topical, personal, or relational issue* needs to be identified. To ensure clarity of thought, it is essential for people to identify and stay on one issue at a time.

Since people gather information through their senses, the second zone is a *fact-finding* area. What do people see, hear, touch, taste, or smell that provides the data for the development of the issue? Knowing the facts gives understanding to the issue.

Third, people develop *thoughts* based on the way they interpret the data they gather through their senses. From these thoughts, expectations are created, which lead to reactions or behavior.

One of the reactions that these interpretations and thoughts invoke are *emotions*. This is the fourth zone. Emotions are a reflection of the mind and are actually more rational than thoughts because they are always consistent with thoughts, whereas thoughts can be irrational depending upon the accuracy and interpretation of facts.

Thoughts and emotions create desire. The fifth zone addresses what we *want* for ourselves, our spouses, and others. It is important for spouses to know one another's desires. It is impossible to meet needs and dreams apart from this knowledge.

The final zone deals with the development of *a plan* that is consistent with the previous zones. It reviews past unsuccessful efforts to resolve the issue, and establishes a current method for pursuing resolution to the issue or realization of a desire the issue prompted.

When issues are important to you, it is wise to first work through these zones alone to ensure a complete personal understanding of *your* issue and to devise a plan consistent with reaching *your* desires or goals. Only then is your understanding of the issue ready to be shared with your spouse. The more you understand your issue, the better you will be able to communicate that issue to your spouse, who can assist you in accomplishing the plan. However, if your partner doesn't possess good listening or understanding skills, the shared pieces of your thoughts and desires will remain a disconnected puzzle.

"He Said, She Said"—Understanding Skills

The goal of listening is to understand an issue from the perspective of the one providing the information. This requires listening skills that force an individual to put his or her own perspective temporarily on the shelf. A regular hindrance to effective communication is interrupting the speaker to inject personal input. To interrupt is to suggest to the speaker that you don't care about the speaker's perspective. Good decisions can never be reached without complete understanding. Interruptions break the speaker's train of thought and prevent the speaker from revealing fully how he or she understands *his* or *her* issue. Interruption is a trigger for conflict.

Five listening skills can help the listener stay focused on what the speaker is saying. If these skills are followed consistently, the information you receive from your spouse will provide data for meeting needs, give opportunities to find common interests, enhance opportunities for encouragement, and build trust, confidence, and intimacy into your relationship.

The first responsibility of a listener is to *pay close attention to the information being sent.* It is important for the listener to note the zone (issue, data gathering, thoughts, emotions, desires, or plan) from which your spouse is speaking. In this way, you, the listener, can ensure that all the zones have been covered and that the information sent is complete.

Second, a good listener shows that he or she is *interested in the conversation* through verbal and nonverbal gestures. A nod of the head, a smile, and the expression in the eyes speak louder than any words about your interest in understanding the pieces that shape your spouse's experiences and perspectives. Verbal remarks like, "that seems incredible," "really," "I'm sorry," or "it's okay" let your spouse know that you are in touch with the message.

Third, a good listener *encourages the speaker to explain further.* In conversation, people tend to hold things back until they are sure the listener is really interested. To overcome this hesitancy on the part of your spouse and to seek more information, you can say, "Is there anything else you heard?" "What other emotions might you be experiencing?" or "Any other desires or suggestions?" As you pay close attention to the zones (listening skill one), opportunities for asking good "further-detail type" questions more readily present themselves.

After the speaker has completed describing his or her awareness of an issue, it is good for the listener to *summarize the speaker's perspective.* This gives both the speaker and listener (the couple) the opportunity to see if the message has been delivered and received accurately. If the summary reveals a misunderstanding, the speaker is given the opportunity to explain further until the listening spouse's summary matches what the speaking spouse is trying to communicate. Remember, you must be committed to understanding the issue from your spouse's perspective.

Fifth, a good listener should use open-ended questions whenever there is a need to gain descriptive information. Open-ended questions are those that begin with *who, what, when, where,* and *how.* They require more than a simple yes or no answer. Try to avoid asking questions that begin with the word *why* because these questions tend to sound argumentative, as if the speaker's thoughts and feelings are suspect.

These speaking and listening skills are essential to any growing relationship, especially for a couple who is trying to navigate the long and twisting roads that comprise a successful marriage marathon. If spouses sincerely want to help each other grow, these skills open the door to personal, topical, and relational disclosure. They provide a path into the puzzle that each caring spouse wants to disclose and longs to understand. The picture desired is definitely worth as many words as it takes.

Message Meltdown—Communication Stoppers

Certain statements not only depict a selfish heart, but also bring vulnerability *with* risk to greater heights. The following remarks block open communication between people and imply a certain amount of superiority of one person over another. People who perceive or experience these remarks as par for the course are generally unable to express their true thoughts and feelings. Eventually they end up defeated, frustrated, discouraged, and angry. Couples who practice these "communication stoppers" find their hopes evaporating like mist in a desert sun. Marriage is hard; making it harder by wounding one or both of its players is relational suicide.

Probably the worst and most condescending of these "stoppers" is the expression "shut up." Very few other phrases do more to damage a person's self-esteem. It should be torn from the vocabulary of every person who desires peace in any kind of relationship (this goes for any type of vulgarity as well). Other ways we belittle people with our tongues are through statements like "Don't bother me now!" or "Not now, I'm watching the game." If something else is important at that moment, ask your spouse if he or she can wait a minute or two; however, there is very little excuse for putting a program or a game before the concerns of one's family and friends. Mute buttons were designed for the television, not for loved ones.

Other statements that hinder communication and reflect an inability to place the needs of others before our own are "Can't you understand anything?" "Can't you say anything right?" "You're such a nag!" "Here we go again!" or "You're so silly." Silliness is often synonymous with foolishness. Still more damaging remarks are "That's not important!" "You're always overreacting," and "You can't help; this is too important!"

Statements like these do nothing to encourage personal or relational growth in those we say we love. Repercussions from these remarks can cause damage that lasts for years and, quite possibly, for a lifetime. A thirteen-year-old boy goes into the garage to ask his father if he can do anything to help him with a construction project. The father, not intentionally wanting to hurt the boy, responds, "No, son. This is too important." For nearly twenty years one young man was afraid of doing anything that would be considered important or challenging because he believed he was incapable of doing anything of real value. It is appropriate to be a builder and shaper of things as long as you always remember that you are foremost a builder and shaper of people.

Saying What You Mean—
General Rules of Communication

It is vitally important to remember seven basic guidelines to good communication.

1. Ask questions. Asking questions shows interest and invokes further disclosure. Though most questions should be open-ended, an occasional closed-ended question beginning "Do you . . . ?" or "Are you . . . ?" may be needed.

2. Don't be defensive, and don't lead. Fear of change is usually the reason for being defensive. Remember, no one is ever right about everything! Also, don't use remarks that lead a speaker to your own conclusion like, "But don't you think . . . ?"

3. Extrasensory perception (ESP) has nothing whatsoever to do with good communication. If you can guess what your spouse means fifty percent of the time, then you have a fifty percent chance of offending him or her. The odds don't give ESP the nod! Successful marathons and marriages are based on effective communication, not intuition!

4. Your understanding of the issue is to be temporarily put on the shelf until your spouse has completed expressing his or her understanding of the issue. If you are truly interested in meeting the needs of your partner, the full disclosure of your spouse's understanding will influence what your view of the issue becomes. Because partners generally want what each other wants, adjustments in the understanding of an issue can occur willingly. Spouses are not in competition to see who makes the most right decisions. Collaboration (the blending of two ideas into one) is the best procedure for reaching objectives.

5. Don't expect your spouse to understand you; be revealing. Sometimes you may think that because your spouse loves you, he or she will naturally know what you want. This is not

generally the case, especially with task-oriented individuals. A caring and loving spouse is glad to help as long as he or she knows what task you want done. To expect your loving spouse to know and act upon your whims, wishes, and wants without discussion and direction is hopeful, but rather unrealistic and risky.

6. Be respectful at all times. Nothing is ever gained by trimming your spouse down to size with barber's shears or chopping him or her off at the knees with a battle-ax. The marriage marathon is a mutual effort, a team activity; it is amazing how often we forget this simple fact.

7. A good relationship is one that works through difficulties so that they don't escalate, not one that avoids difficulty. A couple who would rather avoid difficulties than face them sooner or later discovers that the difficulties have all gathered together as allies to confront the couple with an all-out invasion. The couple usually loses badly! Difficulties suggest a need for change, and mutually agreed upon change usually promotes relational growth.

Talking together makes living together purposeful and productive. It especially provides couples with a means through which they can maintain trust, confidence, and intimacy. The guidelines we have discussed in this chapter protect a couple from making remarks to one another that are inconsistent with the marriage marathon strategy statements. There are enough potholes along the journey; to create your own wastes precious time and energy that can be used more productively to strengthen, rather than frustrate, your union.

CHAPTER 12

Understanding the Power of Forgiveness

$\mathcal{W}$hen Gary was dating his wife, he and his friend Marc would pack up Marc's white Volkswagen bug and travel Interstate 40 from Ozark, Arkansas, to Marietta, Georgia, to see Kathie during breaks from college. On the bug's final journey, Gary was admonished by his friend to remind him to check the oil before starting back from Marietta. In a daze (Gary was going to see the woman he loved), Gary told him, "No problem." Well, at that time, it wasn't.

After a great week in Georgia, Marc and Gary started their journey back to school. They reached an area just outside of Somerville, Tennessee, when they both heard the most awful sound—next to an explosion—that a car can make. In case you haven't guessed, the engine seized up due to lack of oil. As the car came to a stop at the side of the road, the silence was so loud it hurt. Gary knew what his friend was thinking, and he knew what Gary was thinking.

"You didn't remind me, Gary."

"It's not my car, Marc. My memory was deadened by the effects of love."

Oh, we forgot to tell you what happened. If it had been any other fluid besides oil, that little car could have been on the road in a matter of hours. Now it's buried somewhere in a Tennessee wrecking yard. Just like that Volkswagen, marriage can go through a lot and bounce back in a short period of time, but without forgiveness, it dies and gets buried in city hall's file of marital has-beens. Forgiveness, rather than romance, is the oil in the machinery of marriage; forgiveness keeps the gears of communication from seizing up. Without it, relationships stop cold.

Overcoming an Injury

Because people are imperfect and have a naturally selfish inclination to overcome, forgiveness is a necessary part of the marital equation. When one spouse commits an offense or injury against the other, pain ensues, a debt is created, and a natural desire to repay pain for pain becomes the sentence if justice is to be served. Forgiveness is an act that grants an acquittal and vanquishes debts. No longer does the spouse want to repay debt for debt. How does this act take place?

When an offense occurs, marriage is divided into two parties. The offense is the wall that separates the couple. On one side of the wall is the offender, the person who caused the injury; on the other side of the wall is the offended, the person who was hurt and desires justice. If the relationship is going to be restored, *both parties must want the relationship to continue.* A relationship cannot be developed in a courtroom.

Relationships will not be restored by getting even or by repaying debt for debt. No one can actually undo the consequences of an injury by perpetrating an injury on the offender. All that results is that both parties are injured. In marriage, to repay with further injury is actually hurting oneself. The idea is to *restore the union* before further damage is done; in this sense, forgiveness is an act of encouragement. Restoration is accomplished through forgiveness: the canceling of a debt.

When the offense is committed, the offender needs forgiveness. If the relationship is to be spared the added damage of injury brought on by a desire for revenge, the offended spouse must always be ready to forgive. A request for forgiveness places the offender in the position of the breaker of fellowship and the offended as the holder of fellowship. It may seem a bit unfair that the person who was injured is handed the responsibility for the continuance or demise of the relationship, but that is the reality of forgiveness. It's as if the couple is standing on a tennis court, each partner on different sides of the net. The offender serves the ball of forgiveness to the offended, who makes the decision whether or not to play. The offender needs forgiveness to be returned so that the couple can once again work together as a team in a loving relationship. If the offended party is open to making the return, the ball is hit back and the relationship is restored.[1] The consequences of the injury do not become greater, and the couple continues pursuing one another's welfare.

It is true that forgiveness can open the door to manipulation and spouse abuse. However, if the offending spouse admits wrongdoing as an expression of commitment to the welfare of his or her spouse, it is unlikely that the offending spouse will perpetually commit the same offense. The strategies discussed throughout this book don't tolerate manipulation and spouse abuse. The application of these same strategies gives spouses the courage to live in such a way that a forgiven offense is never again brought up to harm or be used against one another. Caring spouses don't want to hurt each other, but occasionally offenses take place.

The line from the movie *Love Story* that permeated our culture and beliefs about love was "Love means never having to say you're sorry." The saying is sentimental, *but it is dead wrong*. In marriage, true love acknowledges the mistakes we make and the hurt we cause each other. True love means having to say, "I'm sorry." Forgiveness is ever present in the relationship, like oil in an automobile, always ready to respond when called upon to ensure that the mistakes couples make are not compounded by further mistakes. The willingness to forgive is a *mind set of two people* who want the best for each other.[2]

Those of us who profess faith in Jesus Christ must always remember the position we have in Christ. Once we were spiritually dead and under the punishment of the law because of the debts we created by sinning against it (Rom. 3:19–20; 5:12–14), but now, through acceptance of His death for our debt, we have been forgiven and have been blessed with eternal life (Rom. 5:15–21; Col. 2:13–14). How can we, who have been forgiven so much, not forgive those who express regret and request forgiveness for the injury they have caused us? May we open our arms, as Christ did on the cross, and be willing to take the pain that others cast our way. If we don't, meaningful relationships may be lost to selfish retribution. "Just as the Lord forgave you, so also should you" (Eph. 4:32; Col. 3:12–13).

Balancing Forgiveness and Trust

There seems to be a great deal of confusion among couples about forgiveness. Often too much is attached to the term. A wife comes to a counselor frustrated that she is not able to trust her husband. To save some money, Chris misled his wife, Gail, about the quality of some tires he bought for their tandem bicycle. His bad judgment caused a blowout and, consequently, an injury to his wife. He says that if she genuinely forgave him, she would not insist on accompanying him to purchase tires to ensure that he doesn't cut corners again. Although she believes that she forgave him, she wonders if she really did—she is still unwilling to let him go alone to make a purchase that has anything to do with their bicycle.

Actually there are two issues here: one is forgiveness, the other, trust. Whenever an offense occurs, trust deteriorates. The longer an offense goes unforgiven, the more damage is done to trust. When forgiveness takes place, *it is wrong* to assume that trust survived at the same level as before the offense; this is seldom the case. Forgiveness takes care of the legal requirement for restoring the relationship, but it *does not* restore the trust. Trust is restored through the reestablishment of open channels of communication and a return to *consistent* care. *Forgiveness is immediate, trust takes time.* Forgiveness provides the opportunity to restore relational growth; trust is the fragile product that comes from restoring the marriage marathon's strategies after an offense occurs.

The wife mentioned above had forgiven her spouse, that is, *she did not want to cause him any harm*; however, her lack of trust in his integrity was a consequence of his own action. Time is needed to rebuild shaken trust. Love for his wife suggests that this man accept the consequence of his actions and act in a way that will restore his wife's confidence. Therefore, the problem was not in the wife, but in the husband. His renewed commitment to protecting his wife would bring about the solution—restored trust. Though the relationship had been restored through forgiveness (it could now grow again), the level of trust lost from his act had to be rebuilt. Although the husband's bad decision caused a blowout, the wife's forgiveness allows the couple to move on in the marriage marathon even though she may have some difficulty trusting him the next time they encounter steep hills or sharp corners.

Forgiveness: Always Available

In one situation, an offense is committed, and the offender wants both to take responsibility for the offense and bring restoration. In another situation, an offense is committed for which the offender wants neither to take responsibility for his actions nor bring restoration. These scenarios can depict situations in both friendships and marriages. Can forgiveness by the offended party be legitimately offered in both situations? Most people tend to answer yes in the first scenario and no in the second. They reason that forgiveness cannot be offered to someone who is unwilling to receive it and who is not interested in restoration. From a theological and legal perspective, however, God always forgives anyone who is willing to admit responsibility for a wrong. His arms are always open and ready to receive a child who has strayed even when His forgiveness is not wanted. Forgiveness is always available, but it is not always received and, therefore, restoration of the relationship is impossible. From this perspective, forgiveness can obviously be offered in both situations.

We must remember that forgiveness, in the legal sense, involves an unwillingness to return pain for pain received, and that forgiveness does not restore trust in a relationship, but only provides the opportunity for its restoration. The availability of forgiveness in the second situation may not renew a friendship, but it does free the offended party from the clutches of the offender. An understanding that trust is the product of dual or reciprocal effort (the love of two people for each other) allows the offended party to accept the failure of the friendship without experiencing undue guilt. There is also no need to harbor anger, although disappointment in the loss of a relationship is understandable. A forgiving spirit allows the offended party to move freely throughout the community without taking different streets and shopping in different stores to avoid the offender. He or she has done all that can be done to restore the friendship. Friendship requires two people equally devoted to its success. You can't be friends with everyone, but forgiveness allows you to be friendly to all, even to a spouse who has brought into a mutually satisfying marriage marathon what you hope is only a temporary delay.

The Product of Love

Trust is the product of applied strategies lived consistently over time; forgiveness is the product of love. Without unconditional love, a person is not willing to sacrifice his or her own rights to relieve another of a debt. If we are unable to forgive, then we are unable to love, for in forgiveness all the benefits of love are realized. Imagine a tropical island covered with palm trees. Forgiveness is not the island, it is the palm trees that provide the shelter under which good things survive hazardous elements. Forgiveness grows out of a heart of love and provides protection and restoration in the lives of couples who want to experience all that love has to offer. In an imperfect world, nothing can grow without the palm trees (forgiveness). In the marriage marathon, forgiveness functions as a road crew repairing areas along the course where love, honor, and encouragement have been removed from the surface. In the truest sense of the word, forgiveness is a mixture of love, honor, and encouragement willingly offered to fill holes that threaten to sidetrack an otherwise successful journey.

Consequences

The pain of consequences comes not from a lack of forgiveness; pain is the natural corollary of doing wrong. Some mistakes must work themselves out, as in the situation where the husband misled his wife about the quality of the tires he purchased for their bicycle. In time, the hurt or pain diminishes, the memory and effects from a past injustice fade away, and trust deepens, even in cases where poor decisions cause physical injury. In these cases, a mistake is remembered in a physical scar that can never be removed; forgiveness and trust, however, ensure that the presence of the scar does not deny the offender the benefits of love. In a healthy relationship, the presence of a physical scar reminds the couple of the struggles they were able to overcome and the changes that they endured to have a meaningful and productive marriage. Some unfortunate actions or behaviors often threaten a marriage; however, loving partners assure that they finish the course together! The restoration in the relationship comes because the presence of an *emotional scar* has been removed by an act of selfless love—forgiveness.

CHAPTER 13

Bringing Style into the Journey

*O*ften, when we think of style, we think of the way in which things are done. In communication, this means thinking about how things are said. Researchers tell us that a person's understanding of another's discussion is seven percent what is said and ninety-three percent how the message is delivered.[1] This makes style a critical part of the communication process. It is like saying, "Of course I'm concerned about Lindsay's education," while my back is turned to my wife as I continue working on the lawnmower. The context in which the message is delivered is more telling than the content. Often, actions do speak louder than words!

Though a brief discussion of personality types—like the very entertaining one designed by John Trent, using animals to identify different personalities—could be used in a section like this, the focus here is on how people in general communicate to others.[2] Although their personalities describe the different characteristics people have (aggressive, passive, playful, or loyal), we are looking at communication similarities in all personalities that influence and threaten our ability to communicate in an other-centered fashion. Differences in personality do not preclude selfish expression or styles of communication that are unique to gender, though personalities tend to shape or color them. Every personality consists of communication styles that are created by gender differences, manipulation, and routine. This section looks at communication issues that are common to all personalities.

Because the manner in which couples speak to one another is so important to a marriage, we need to develop tools that will enhance the way we deliver messages. No one wants the content of his or her message to be misunderstood. If how we deliver a message is paramount to ensuring accuracy, then communications skills must be learned. Better understanding of how individuals gather data, awareness of how the sexes communicate, control of our motives and gestures, openness to flexibility, and a willingness to pause and reflect on priorities will go a long way toward helping us keep the needs of our spouses in focus. To allow for vulnerability and honesty, we must communicate in a style that is spouse-centered.[3]

Gender-Related Styles of Communication

Gender, Grammar, and Gutturals

Research has shown that women speak, on average, twice as many words as men (a 2 to 1 ratio; 25,000 per day versus 12,500).[4] This accounts for the communication letdown in men at the end of the day. If a man has a job that requires personal interaction, it is likely that he will be talked out by the end of the day. Without some type of reprieve, a husband may be unable to communicate well with his wife in the evening—a behavior that is often interpreted as lack of interest in the relationship. On the other hand, a wife's ability to communicate in the evening may be seen by her husband as pressure, especially when his lack of participation is interpreted as disinterest in the relationship. A conflict ensues, both wondering why the other has a problem.

From childhood on, women use words to describe their thoughts and feelings. They hold full conversations with people and things from the moment they can speak. Men, on the other hand, are a little bit different. While 60 percent of the time they use words, the other 40 percent of the time they express themselves through sounds known as gutturals.[5] Tim Allen, star of the situation comedy "Home Improvement," has mastered the art of this male phenomenon. It's not that men can't develop good vocabularies, they simply enjoy adding some flavor to their conversations. Men tend to be less conversational, preferring to get to the point and move on to something else that doesn't always require in-depth discussion: a game, a hobby, or social events that accept grunting. As a result, conversational women find men disinterested in lengthy discussion, especially ones that deal with relationships. Most men prefer to solve issues quickly and move on. In the context of a relationship, this can be quite offensive to women.

What is the cause behind these different styles of communication that seem to be linked to gender? Why does it happen? A male fetus experiences a testosterone bath over the brain at about the twenty-sixth week of pregnancy. This bath eliminates thousands upon thousands of fibers that connect the right hemisphere to the left. Some believe that this bath is what creates these differences between the genders. Women are more whole-brained, which makes them more relational, while men are less-connected, making them more deductive and solutions-oriented. Men tend to see things more in black and white, while women tend to see things more connected or interrelated. This may also account for a woman being more in touch with her emotions. This physical fact makes men and women unique and is the cause for much of the confusion between the sexes.[6]

Men and Women: A Different Approach

Men and women see many things differently or at least lean toward different focal points. Some of the areas that particularly relate to problems associated with marriage include (1) how they view being right, (2) what they prefer to discuss, (3) how they understand the use of words, (4) how they view language, (5) how they tend to listen, (6) how they respond to problems, (7) what attitudes they have toward apologizing, and (8) what attitudes they have toward conflict.

For a man, *being right* is a strong desire that colors much of the way he interacts with people. A man not only wants his spouse to understand his thoughts, he wants her to agree with him. A woman, though not desiring to be wrong, places greater emphasis on being heard and understood. She wants her spouse to *validate her thoughts* even if he does not necessarily agree. If she is wrong, she is willing to admit it and continue on unless her husband creates an environment that belittles the way she thinks.

Men prefer to talk about *things,* whereas women, being more relational, favor conversations about *people;* men will talk more about what they know rather than who they know. A man cares about those with whom he works, but doesn't desire to spend time talking about his co-workers unless they assist or hinder him in reaching his goals. Women consider knowledge about the lives of those with whom they work important. Men may not talk as quickly or as easily as do women about their personal lives and children, especially with people they don't know.

Women seem to see *meaning behind the words,* while men generally *mean exactly what they say.* A father might tell his daughter after she returns from a ten-day trip that he doesn't want her staying up late listening to music anymore. While she was away, he was able to get some extra sleep that was appreciated. The wife, overhearing this conversation, tells her husband that it was mean to tell his daughter that things were better with her not around. He stares in amazement and responds, "I didn't say things were better when she was gone. I said I don't want her playing music after I go to sleep because I need and appreciate the rest." This difference is very important; a man needs to ask questions and summarize his wife's statements to ensure accuracy. A woman needs to summarize to ensure she is not hearing things her husband did not say.

For men, language or discussion is used *to compete, to compare,* or *to challenge.* Men are generally concerned about doing things right, and they love to make their victories known. For women, language is used to *express a caring attitude;* they use language to bring others into a conversation. Language is used to gain information more for understanding than for competition.

When it comes to listening, a man's *competitive* nature and desire to be right demands that he take a course in listening. Men love to interrupt. Because their point of view is very important to them, they have a tendency to be defensive. Because women need to establish relationships, listening skills are willingly received. Women use listening as a way to *respond* caringly to people.

Because men are goal-oriented and like to be right, *they usually handle problems rather aggressively.* Men always seem to have advice, an answer to every problem. But this trait can work against men in relationships. When a wife wants to talk about a problem she's having, more times than not, all she is looking for is a listening ear. Before she can finish voicing her concerns, her husband interrupts with advice. Although he often sees himself as simply trying to help his wife out of a jam, he leaves her bewildered and her thoughts invalidated. Her willingness to share other concerns is, therefore, weakened. If his wife doesn't let him know her reaction, he leaves the conversation believing he has loved his wife by having the right answer at the right time. His wife, however, leaves the conversation hurt and wondering what has gone wrong in the relationship. Women *approach problems empathetically,* wanting to know more and provide assistance if asked. A woman tends to become a part of the solving process rather than the one with all the answers.

Men *don't like to apologize;* it implies that they don't understand something or that they have made a mistake. This unfortunate quality is not helpful in establishing relationships with women, who tend to *apologize much more easily*. When relationships matter, apologies help to keep the peace. It is only after a woman has been misused many times that her willingness to make an apology comes less frequently or disappears. Failure to a man is often considered an inability to take care of those to whom he has committed himself. Men are incredibly vulnerable relationally because relationships offer challenges that are not always black and white. When a woman reacts harshly to what she sees as an indifferent and insensitive husband, she risks closing doors to relational growth. She needs to work at understanding her husband's relational quirks and flaws and to guide him with patience and loving concern. It is important for men to understand that apologizing to their wives does not mean failure, that it is okay to make a mistake. Society is very hard on people who make mistakes; married couples can't afford to be the same way. Men also need to understand and remember that not everything is solved quickly nor even needs their involvement. Women want a friend and a listener; they aren't always looking for a problem solver.

Although conflict is extremely detrimental to relationships, men *tend to be right at home* with it. Could this have something to do with their desire to win and be right all the time? Probably so! Women, on the other hand, would generally prefer to *avoid conflict* rather than pursue it. Since winning the argument isn't the driving force behind an argument, they don't have a lot of desire to be involved in one.

Understanding how men and women communicate differently can help spouses respond to each other's stylistic idiosyncrasies with patience. The more we understand these differences, the less surprised and shocked we are when they arise. We also misinterpret our spouses' statements and reactions less frequently. Understanding these differences helps us all to be more spouse-centered.[7]

Communication Chaos—
Manipulative Styles of Communication

Unfortunately, certain styles of communication are used to manipulate others to one's own point of view. These styles are completely inconsistent with marriage-marathon strategies designed to protect a marriage. They are often secretive, demanding, controlling, unloving, and at their core, selfish. To some degree, at least one of these styles plays havoc in each of our lives. Neither sex corners the market on destructive communication styles—it's an area in which sexual equality truly has been achieved!

People with the first of four manipulative styles of communication are known as the Silent Stuffers. These people long to be alone. Something in their lives has caused them to seek isolation. They *avoid conflict and behave like they have no emotions.* They store a lot inside, but very few people know about their personal struggles, not even their spouses. They manipulate through a subtle martyr-type personality, often draining others of their sympathy. Sometimes this style is evidenced by a calm disapproval and hidden hatred of the world around them. Marriage to a Silent Stuffer makes participation in the marriage marathon lonely and tiresome. You know you're moving, but you're never sure where you're going.

The second type are the Cool Crushers. Their claim to fame is their ability to stay calm in the midst of difficulty. They never admit to being either disturbed or happy. When conflict is taking place, they remain undisturbed by the whole affair until the opportunity arrives to deliver a *well-controlled, cool crushing blow* to their victims. Their remarks are never said in the heat of emotional rage, but are just as damaging to the victims. When the damage is done, they calmly go about their business as if nothing significant has occurred. Marriage to a Cool Crusher makes the marriage marathon unsettling and eerie. You know that your bicycle's seat is going to fall off, but you don't know why or when.

Demolition Directors plan the conflict in which they are going to unleash a round of calculated emotion that is sure to bring the conflict to an immediate close. They wait for their moment, pretending to listen to the view of their victims, while all the time planning their quick and decisive rebuttal. Like Cool Crushers, they are rational and very good thinkers who are able to manipulate every situation for personal gain. The difference between Demolition Directors and Cool Crushers is the *intensity* of their calculated attacks. Demolition Directors calmly plan conflict that is unleashed in a fury of emotion that is sure to squelch any resistance to their desires. Marriage to a Demolition Director makes the marriage marathon intimidating and often demeaning. You know a big storm could be around the next bend, one that will leave you soaked, but you have no idea how to avoid it.

The final manipulative characters are identified as Loose Lightnings. They want their way, and everyone knows it at all times. Everything bothers Loose Lightnings, and their explosions occur any time they feel threatened. Emotion is their first name and conflict their last. They strike without warning, leaving their victims singed by flashes of emotional heat. Marriage to a Loose Lightning makes the marriage marathon intolerable and without reward. There are always steep downhill grades, unending inclines, and dead-man curves for which the other partner is always blamed.

Most of us have met one of these manipulative styles. Probably all of us have seen a trace of these styles in someone we love and perhaps in ourselves. Some people exhibit more than one of these selfish characteristics. These attitudes and behaviors may have been copied from others or chosen as an apparent safety net from difficult circumstances. Often, they serve as protection from a world that appears to offer more fear and disappointment than hope.

When they raise their ugly heads in the context of marriage, they leave behind the very things that appear to have created them: fear and disappointment. It is critical that we have the freedom to discuss our personal challenges with our spouses in an environment safe from harmful criticism. These selfish styles are perpetuated by physical, emotional, and mental abuse. Sometimes, winning the marriage marathon isn't nearly as important as surviving it. The more we practice the strategies presented in this book, the less manipulative we will become and the fewer manipulators we will create. No one can develop a healthy personal life or meaningful relationships with a selfish, demanding, controlling, or manipulative style of communication.

Routine Styles of Communication

Two criteria describe routine styles of communication: extended patterns of activity and extended stimuli-activated negative behavior. Don't ride off! These may sound a bit technical, but understanding them can keep your participation in the marriage marathon from turning into a long and boring transit across a desert of familiarity. Let's briefly look at these two negative styles of communication.

Do you ever feel like your marriage could use an overhaul? This is the first sign that your marriage is caught in a rut developed through *patterns of activity that have become routine.* Even though your marriage has a nice hum to it, it is the same hum that's been there for the past five years. You just keep on doing what seems comfortable and natural regardless of how boring and unstimulating it may be. You're peddling as much as ever but the scenery never seems to change—you're going in circles. You don't like it and you even complain from time to time, but neither one of you takes the initiative to change courses. You have become comfortable with the familiar. The mountains, valleys, rivers, and forests all look like never-ending plains. You're stuck in a rut, the pressure in both tires is low, and rust has started to develop on the frame of your bicycle.

If you become frustrated with your spouse's behavior but refuse to let him or her know, your spouse's continued practice of the behavior provokes an emotional reaction that eventually becomes a programmed pattern or rut, that is, *a stimuli-activated negative behavior.* Whenever that particular behavior surfaces, emotions automatically reveal themselves. For example, a husband continues to come home twenty to thirty minutes late from work. His wife doesn't like it but decides she doesn't want to express her thoughts and feelings. Gradually, her disappointment escalates into resentment, but still she remains silent. Her husband notices her getting a little distant, but when asked if something is bothering her, she denies any problem. For whatever reason, the husband begins getting home earlier. The wife is pleased, but she notices that every time he enters the door, she resists greeting him and a negative feeling lingers in her heart. She has fallen into a pattern or routine style of communication that expresses itself negatively because she has chosen to remain silent about her husband's past negative behavior. She still harbors unresolved feelings. The stimulus for her behavior is the mere presence of her spouse at the end of the day.

Concealed thoughts and feelings eventually reveal themselves in routine negative behaviors. Unless you disclose and discuss these negative thoughts and feelings, they will spiral down, deepen with time, and become a normal part of the way in which you and your spouse interact. Sometimes patiently *putting up* with an annoying behavior in your spouse leads to your being *put out* with him or her. If you do not appreciate a particular behavior in your spouse, don't conceal it "for the sake of love." In fact, it is because you love your spouse that you must disclose and discuss the annoyance so that the product of concealed thoughts and feelings (resentment) does not settle into your relationship. If you choose not to disclose your negative thoughts and feelings, the reasons for them and for your negative attitude toward your spouse can become clouded by the passage of time and routine, producing a serious hindrance to your hope of riding a successful marathon. Your partner is left frustrated and confused, not knowing what he or she has done or what can be done to remedy the problem. Just like in the previous style (routine patterns of activity), you're stuck in a rut.

Relational Ruts: A Definition

What is a relational rut? It is defined as a "fixed or established behavior that governs daily interaction; a fixed or established way of acting, especially one that is boring and monotonous."[8] It is reactive in that it responds to the same stimuli day in and day out. It is instantaneous because it always responds the same way; it is a pattern because it never changes; and it is directive because it determines the future, possibly forever. Relational ruts can be seen in our attitudes toward sexual activity. Ruts are revealed when we have the same emotional reaction to a daily meeting, travel the same streets to get to work each day, follow a particular mental process to complete an activity day after day, or engage in a spiritual experience because it's that time of day. They are the routine, the habits that make life comfortable—very, very comfortable, to the point of boredom. They also create the tedious negative behaviors or attitudes that never seem to go away.

Relational ruts occur in a marriage when we become comfortable with the way things are done or we accept negative behavior. We may try to avoid whatever stimulus provokes our spouses' negative behaviors rather than attempt to identify their causes. When we stop evaluating our interaction, the doldrums and distancing begin. Thinking becomes mechanical, but not creative. Responses are often governed by reactions to past patterns rather than by thoughtful consideration of current realities. Ruts that reflect negative behavior continue methodically; they never seem to go away. Other ruts are not connected to negative behavior; they were originally well thought out and planned ideas, events, and procedures, but over time have become meaningless expressions of time-honored tradition.[9] Even good ideas need an occasional overhaul! Ruts are like rust. If left alone, they gradually eat away love, honor, and encouragement, and erode healthy communication.

Removing Relational Ruts

The first step to removing relationship ruts is *recognizing them.* If you don't identify the ruts that have developed in your marriage, you will remain trapped in routine behavior that continues to bring boredom and build barriers. Everyone can design a great family event that eventually loses its thrill, but should it be maintained for the sake of family tradition or because "that's the way it has always been done"? Or, you may have a problem you believe your spouse won't understand or appreciate, so you choose to keep it private. This choice conceals thoughts and feelings that could create attitudes to which your spouse cannot respond. The longer you conceal the problem and leave it unresolved, the more likely it will produce a lasting negative attitude, that is, a rut. Ruts exist, and many couples get trapped in them. You need to identify them so that you can then remove them.

Three questions help to identify relationship ruts. The first question is, "What areas in our lives never change, or what issues always seem to get the same response behaviorally or emotionally?"

- I drive the kids to school on the same route every day.
- We shop at the same stores.
- We never miss a Sunday morning service.
- We haven't met a new friend in five years.
- We haven't had a vacation more than fifty miles from home in six years.
- Finances seem to get us at each other's throat every month.
- I get stressed every time my parents plan a visit.
- I find myself reading romance novels rather than talking with my spouse.

When activities in your married life become monotonous or when certain topics or issues provoke unhealthy behavioral or emotional responses, your journey is taken over by relationship-stifling ruts rather than shaped by the marriage marathon strategies that are designed to stimulate creativity.

The second question is, "When and how often do these routine events or patterns of behavior take place?" Every morning, or in the evening twice a week? Are dinners always the same—any new recipes lately? How do you react when the stepchildren come for a visit or when a certain neighbor walks by the house? Does tension rise between you and your spouse every time your teenage daughter comes home? Do you get a certain surge of anger whenever your spouse sits down to watch the television? It is important to see if the timing of events is producing the same response again and again. If it is, you are in a rut. Sometimes identifying the timing of a routine reaction (when it takes place) helps to identify the issue as well.

The third question that helps to recognize a rut is, "Where do repetitive behaviors and emotions tend to take place?" Do you generally have the same argument with your spouse in the kitchen before dinner? Does it seem that whenever you get in the car, something is said that makes the drive uncomfortable? Sometimes a place becomes the impetus for a routine difficulty; something negative always seems to occur there. Notice where you spend most of your time and determine what, if any, behaviors seem to be tied to that place. Take time to sit down with your spouse regularly to evaluate your relationship and behaviors so that you can avoid the intrusion of an unwanted routine or relationship rut. It's critical that you pay close attention to each other's evaluation. Ruts are often invisible to those who are their captives.

The second step to removing relationship ruts is to *understand the undercurrents*. What caused the rut? Many emotions are connected with family traditions and methods for handling situations. Often ideas we bring into a marriage have not been thoroughly evaluated. They have been accepted carte blanche. Some passed-on traditions are easier to remove when they become burdensome or problematic because we aren't personally committed to them. However, traditions and ways of doing things that we have adopted because we personally believe in them are more difficult to shed. We must remember that methods are expendable—our spouses are not! Methods must keep up with present demands lest they entangle us in irrelevant routines.

The causes for relationship ruts that reveal themselves as repetitive negative behaviors are more difficult to discover and may require some third-party counseling because they are deeply tied to a person's past. Some of these behaviors can be adjusted by a couple's willingness to sit down together with close family members or friends and safely discuss troubling characteristics and previously hidden difficulties. Often the cause for unresolved relationship ruts is related to a spouse's inability to talk about difficult issues from the past.

The third step to removing relationship ruts demands the *termination of the tedious*. Those of us who are more structured by nature find this step threatening. Not everyone is comfortable with change, but when the marriage marathon is in jeopardy, fear of change must be subordinate to change itself. Changing a discipline method, hair style, apparel trend, or working habit is not easy, but if the change makes your relationship better, your concern for meeting the needs of your spouse should motivate your terminating the unuseful custom. Changing the location of family vacations, driving a different way to work, shopping at a different grocery store from time to time, or moving the furniture around in the house are simple and needed changes that will add a bit of spice. Giving up a bad attitude or a negative behavior generally happens easily in a context where communication is vulnerable, but without risk. Structure doesn't like change, but it is inevitable if people are to move ahead in their lives!

The final step to removing relationship ruts is actually a step that prevents ruts from developing. Each day should be an opportunity to *seek spontaneity*. Plans do not have to be so set in stone that an occasional adjustment can't be made. Flexibility allows freedom to open doors of opportunity and fun that are always present but often passed by because of rigidity. Although too much spontaneity leads to chaos, occasional changes in plan take your marriage out of idle and give it a needed shift. Flexibility allows for change that gives the marriage marathon a sudden acceleration of energy and creates new opportunities.

Relationship ruts represent a style of communication that is often reflected through behavior rather than words. But whether by behavior or words, unnecessary and unhealthy routine leaves participants in the marriage marathon on a perpetual incline that eventually drains them of the energy needed to continue. Sometimes things just have to change!

Changing Your Style of Communication

Changing your style is an intentional act that is not limited by the differences between males and females, the presence of an ingrained manipulative style of communication, or how long you've followed a routine. Change is an act of will that is driven by strategies and principles to which you commit yourself. People decide to change because they believe doing right by others is an obligation, not a preference. The results that stem from doing right (trust, intimacy, stability) are usually not strong enough to bring indefinite change in a person who doesn't believe in the rightness of his or her actions. Your beliefs sway your actions and desires.

Summary and Strategy Progression

A marriage is the product of strong determination based on principles that make communication possible. Every marriage starts with untested love and trust, with vulnerable individuals who hope for openness and friendship. Love and trust do not come because we take wedding vows; love comes as a choice and trust comes as a reward to those who make commitments and live by them. "I will place my spouse's needs before my own." "I will daily love, honor, and encourage my spouse." "I will practice a style of communication that allows my spouse to be vulnerable and honest at all times." These strategies lay the foundation for healthy communication.

People who focus their energy on the concerns of those they love will work to communicate in a style that makes resolving conflict not just a possibility, but an opportunity that leads to growth. Without healthy, spouse-centered communication, conflict goes unresolved and the marriage marathon becomes a spectacle of agony and defeat. The thrill of potential victory is lost in a web of self-preservation and hurt feelings. Love creates an environment for safe communication so that needs can be met and conflicts resolved.

"I will place my spouse's needs before my own."

"I will daily love, honor, and encourage my spouse."

"I will practice a style of communication that allows my spouse to be vulnerable and honest at all times."

You have just passed Marriage Marathon Milestone 3. Keep peddling!

❧ Strategy Four ❧

*I will seek resolution and
growth during conflict.*

Conflict Resolution: Seeking Growth in Times of Conflict

The problem with conflict resolution is that there is generally more conflict than resolution. The differences, both known and unknown, and the level of maturity at the outset of a marriage make conflict inevitable. No couple is ever "just right" for one another, and maturity is a process that is dependent upon openness, honesty, skills, time, and experience. A couple who can't accept and work through their differences and fails to understand and practice the strategies laid out in the previous sections of this book cannot mature in their relationship. As a result, conflict develops and intensifies throughout their marriage until their union becomes no more than a dysfunctional dwelling for disgruntlement and dismay or ends in divorce because of differences considered to be irreconcilable.

At the beginning of the marriage marathon, we tend to see only the good in our partners. We overlook the little things that bother us and generally experience a happy but surreal union. Eventually something occurs that has to be handled; for us or for our spouses, the issue is too important to overlook. We sit at the table and talk about our different perspectives on the issue; neither of us bends; one of us remarks, "I was wondering if the stubbornness I saw in your father was going to show up in you. I guess you're going to be just like him." From this point, an initial disagreement—a minor conflict that could have been used to create relational growth—becomes a topic to be ignored, an argument about some other unrelated issue, or a time of hurt, disappointment, and disillusionment.

To prevent conflict from controlling marriage, strategies must be consistently followed, but often we forget our commitments in the midst of disagreement. Strategies are to a marriage what truth is to the Christian life. In an admonition to the Galatians for allowing false teachers to substitute the truth of liberty in Christ with legalism, Paul wrote, "For in Christ Jesus neither circumcision nor uncircumcision has any value. The only thing that counts is faith expressing itself through love. You were running a good race. Who cut in on you and kept you from obeying the truth?" (Gal. 5:6–8). Similarly, in marriage, the "false teachers" who keep us from obeying God's strategies for marriage are usually ignorance of the strategies and our own sinful nature, which rejects faith and love to serve the flesh or self (Gal. 5:13–26). Paul reminded us that if we "bite and devour one another, take care lest you be consumed by one another" (Gal. 5:15 NASB). Vying to gain an advantage in the spiritual realm or in marriage invokes competition rather than cooperation, and where competition reigns, there must always be a loser—or two!

Conflict is initially an opportunity to identify personal and relational weaknesses. It becomes troubling and divisive when people respond to it negatively or selfishly. Conflict in marriage does not occur because we are perfect; it occurs because we are imperfect, are different from one another, and lack a complete understanding of each other's histories (how we became different). The principles and strategies offered throughout this book are provided to help you create an environment in which you can overcome weaknesses, understand and appreciate differences, and grow together as a couple devoted to each other's welfare. A good marriage is not one that strives for perfection, but one that focuses on the personal and relational growth of its partners. It creates an environment that is forgiving of flaws, sympathetic to sorrow, compassionate in crisis, and calm in conflict.

Though not all disagreements and differences can be quickly resolved, they must never define the potential or limit the longevity of a marriage. You can choose to care for your relationship while you are in the midst of a disagreement.

Steve and Mary gave birth to a child with epilepsy. Attempts to control the seizures through medication were not successful. Mary learned from her doctor that a high fat diet is effective with many young children who suffer from epileptic seizures. Steve, however, was concerned that the diet would not work and might create undue stress for their child. He was reluctant to begin the diet. This scenario had the potential of developing into a relationship-ending conflict, but both Steve and Mary worked with one another, cared for one another, and found a solution that did not lead to the end of their marriage. Mary gathered all the information she could on the subject to help Steve overcome his concerns. She also involved the help of a person Steve respected who could privately listen to and encourage Steve. Their different views (conflict) lasted about six months. Because Mary was patient with Steve, he was able to make the adjustment and support the diet more enthusiastically. What may appear to be unresolvable, in time, finds a solution. It is our commitment to care for one another that makes conflict an occasion for growth rather than a reason to withdraw from the marriage marathon.

Marriage Strategy 4

To create a positive attitude toward conflict, you must first see conflict as a path through which greater intimacy will flow. This strategy statement is designed to instill a positive approach to conflict: *"I will seek resolution and growth during conflict."* Couples who accept the previous strategy statements and the principles associated with them already have the background to make a commitment to this fourth strategy statement.

Without a commitment to focus on the needs of your spouse, you cannot accept the differences that surface as the marriage progresses. Without a commitment to love, honor, and encourage your spouse, your marriage will lack the patience and tolerance needed for resolving conflict. Without vulnerability or honest communication, conflict will shut down the openness that you need to reveal your inner puzzle and grow, and without spouse-centered communication, differences create Olympic-sized challenges rather than team efforts. Each strategy statement builds on the previous statements to make handling conflicts a realistic and positive challenge rather than something that stifles your dreams. Conflict is unhealthy or destructive when the strategies of marriage are ignored. The healthy and constructive resolution of conflict succeeds in a marriage marathon that operates in accordance with these strategies.

CHAPTER 14

Peddling Softly Through the Minefields

*A*lthough it is very important that we view conflict in marriage as an occasion for growth, it is critical that we also understand the consequences of unresolved conflict. When we find it difficult to discuss our differences, eventually we will find ourselves in a relationship that is personally destructive. Initially unresolved conflict creates anxiety and stress. Because we stop talking about critical issues, we gradually become isolated from each other and seek to find consolation in outside interests or with other people. We become uncertain about the future, and are fearful for our emotional, mental, and physical welfare.[1] If some resolution is not discovered, emotional stress can lead to physical or mental illness.[2]

Because parents are the initial influence on a child's ability to learn productive coping skills, the inability or unwillingness to resolve conflict in a marriage can impair a child's ability to have a successful marriage. "One of the main causes of neurotic parent-child relationships is the neurotic husband-wife relationship. Treatment for children's problems often requires helping the parents to learn better ways to learn and love."[3] Ken Canfield discovered that "marital failure among sexual offenders was one of the distinguishing characteristics that led to the sexual abuse of children."[4] Unresolved marital conflict can have horrendous consequences.

When you are unable to resolve conflict with your spouse due to your ignorance of relationship skills, your behavior borders on neglect; the unwillingness to resolve conflict is paramount to mental and physical abuse. It may appear to be overly simplistic to say that the admonition to "love one's spouse" is the antidote to societal anarchy, however it should be understood that solutions do not need to be as complex as the conflicts that beg for them. A loving attitude and a few simple principles and skills can lessen the intensity of marital conflict by clearing a more peaceful path through a jungle that always seems to be closing in on all sides. Identifying the principles and skills for conflict resolution is the purpose of this section.

Handling Emotion

Your ability to respond positively and productively to your spouse during a difficult situation is directly related to your ability to control your emotions. Though there are some arguments over the place of emotion in relationship to cognition (which comes first?),[5] it seems rather obvious that emotions are largely based on one's *understanding* of a situation (chronic depression, which may be more closely linked to a genetic disorder, is an exception[6]). Emotion is an affective reaction (feeling) that stems from the interpretation of information retrieved through the senses.[7] People who are able to control their emotional reaction in difficult situations help keep productive lines of communication open. Therefore, they participate in focused discussions that develop faster resolution and lasting resolve.

When you are angry or disappointed over a decision or action made by your spouse, you don't have to deny your emotions. You can be angry or disappointed without "letting it all hang out" or attacking your spouse either verbally or physically. Such attacks are destructive to relationships. Love for a spouse can never be conditional: "I will love you as long as you don't upset me." It is essential that spouses remember their commitments to one another at all times, especially *during* conflict. Your spouse needs to know when something he or she says or does angers, hurts, or disappoints you. This awareness helps spouses adjust to each other and grow together.

On the other hand, your spouse does not need reciprocal treatment. Your pain does not require that you give an equal dose of pain to your spouse. Those who live by the policy of returning hurts find their emotions and relationships spiraling out of control. To keep conflict from being destructive, you need to consider whether you are expressing your emotions in an other-centered or self-centered way. Ask yourself, "Are my emotions expressed to satisfy my own needs or are they expressed to bring understanding and restitution to our union?" How you answer this question determines the intensity with which conflict will be experienced.

Unchecked Emotions: The Source of Marital Conflict

Most conflicts are intensified because emotion is unleashed. Disagreements do not inevitably lead to volatility, although some marriages are marked by volatility. Because we lack relationship principles and skills, have not experienced healthy relationships in our family of origin or with our friends, and are culturally driven to make decisions based on how we feel, emotion has become the foundational factor in determining and justifying our actions and behaviors. The vast majority of us make decisions based on emotion—how external circumstances affect our feelings. Our lives are dominated by the opinions and feelings of those around us rather than by our own perception of ourselves and our understanding of a particular issue. We are influenced rather than influencing. We are emotionally driven rather than intellectually or thoughtfully driven.[8]

Car dealers are well aware of the cultural tendency to make decisions based on how we feel rather than on what is right or is factual. They always ask the potential buyer about feelings: "How does the color make you feel?" "Doesn't that stereo have a great sound?" "How do those seats feel to you?" They might even make comments about how good the buyer looks in the car. After all, a buyer wants to feel good about his or her purchase. Then the dealers offer a purchase plan that can fit any budget, even a budget that reflects bad credit. People will not buy something that doesn't make them feel good. Too many decisions are made on car lots based on emotion independent of reality, need, and common sense. The result is often disappointment, extended debt, and dismay. The same process takes place in marriage. A husband forgets to bring home a loaf of bread from the store. His wife feels angry about his forgetfulness and immediately calls him "stupid, uncaring, and unthoughtful." The result: one unthoughtful act spawns another and then another.

Those who express emotions without considering the consequences can create growing and unrelenting conflict. Because we fail to consider the repercussions of our actions or think about the best or most constructive way to handle our emotions, we (as well as those who live and work with us) live anxious and uncertain lives. Our self-esteem diminishes, stress is a catalyst for more severe emotional outbursts, and our lives are controlled by the agendas of others. Reactionaries will always react emotionally to the actions, behaviors, and statements of others. Rather than having a value system of their own through which they process interactions, they respond robot-like to the value systems of others.

On the other hand, those who are thoughtfully driven become more confident in decision making, experience greater self-esteem, and handle stress much better because they evaluate their emotions, measure the consequences of their decisions, and act independently from the agendas of others. Although they do not ignore their emotions, they are careful not to allow positive or negative emotions to make their decisions. Emotions are more productive and positive when they come as the product of a good decision. Though emotions are an important indicator of the way we think and understand life and act as a wonderful guide to discovering our likes and dislikes, they must never be used to make important relationship, career, and financial decisions. Emotions must fall to second place behind a system of strategies and principles that protect us from a reactionary lifestyle.

Critical Choices: A Mental Wrestling Match

Every day we are confronted with numerous mental wrestling matches between misinformation and fact, and the emotion that acts as a pendulum between them. Events take place in our lives that demand a decision. The wrestling match involves the process of gathering accurate information to make an informed decision while at the same time evaluating the emotion that is triggered as a result of the event. If we choose to act too quickly, we may find that the information we responded to may be inaccurate, and the ensuing action we take will be based on what is *perceived* to be right. If we choose to follow the leading of our emotions, the ensuing action or behavior will be based on what *feels* right. If we choose, however, to gather information to make the most informed reaction (decision), our emotions will be under the control of our minds (responsive rather than reactive), and our decision will be based on thoughtful consideration of the facts and be the *best* decision possible. The first two choices allow the event to lead to conflict, while the last choice brings understanding, peace, and resolution.

We are not attempting to diminish the importance of emotions. They are natural and necessary to good mental health. What is being suggested is that most of us tend to give more attention to our feelings than to emotionally detached discussions or reason (thinking). Those of us who are primarily feelers need to be encouraged to think more about our decisions so we can ensure that the best decision is being made. "A person can understand himself and realize his full human potential only if he can both think and feel; an overemphasis on one at the expense of the other will always constitute a characterological handicap."[9]

Good thinking leads to proper emotional responses. Emotional responses at the expense of good thinking create personal conflict that is unnecessary and avoidable. Feelings are a reflection of our thoughts. When we take the time to process information accurately and take into consideration the concerns or needs of our spouses, our emotions become a healthy reflection of the mind. When data are not thought through, our emotions become the catalyst for disruptive and harmful decisions that consider only our own needs at the expense of the needs of others.

Checked Emotions: The Source of Marital Comfort

You can keep your emotions in check. You may feel like being curt or angry with your spouse, but keep in mind that such behavior will be detrimental to both of you. Make decisions based on what you *know* is right, not on what you *feel* is right. Remaining committed to the marriage marathon strategies helps you to calmly express your emotions and discover ways to resolve differences and avoid future ones.

Whenever you sense that disappointment, withdrawal, or anger is getting too strong or out of control, two steps should be taken to channel that emotion so that your response is not detrimental to your relationship. First, you must evaluate the situation. Who is involved and what is the issue? Did your spouse understand everything clearly? Second, consider your own needs and those of your spouse. Taking these two steps in an emotionally charged situation forces you to *pause* and *think*. The moment you ask yourself introspective questions about a divisive issue, your emotions are either held in check or they tend to subside, and your mind can process or consider your commitments (strategies). Executing difficult turns or maneuvering through narrow and treacherous side-streets during a torrential rain of emotion could divert you from the marriage marathon strategies you chose to follow and from considering the consequences of a crash. Keeping your emotions in check helps you to focus and allows your strategies, rather than your emotions, to determine the course of action. The best solution to a problem is arrived at with the needs and interests of both spouses in mind. Unchecked emotions squash vulnerability (openness) and make resolution during conflict improbable. Conflict is inevitable and resolvable—it never has to be divisive or volatile. *Think* about it—you'll be glad you did!

CHAPTER 15

Scouting the
Course Ahead

*A*lthough we can't prepare for marriage by scouting out the course in the same way that cyclists can, there are initiatives we can take that limit the number of potholes and detours we will experience. By discussing issues in advance, establishing parameters for keeping the peace, learning some practical maneuvers for squelching conflict, and reflecting on successes and failures regularly, we can get a clearer view of what will cross our paths on the course ahead.

Identifying Potential Conflicts

A simple way to avoid conflict is to make ourselves aware of potential conflicts that can threaten a marriage. We all approach life differently. Marriage does not automatically alter lifelong habits; it simply brings two different agendas together into a ring to discover whether the ring will be used for boxing or as a symbol of unity. The more you uncover and discuss differences between you and your spouse, the less likely you are to experience extended and frustrating conflict. Before discussing nine potential conflicts in greater detail, the following list of questions will help you identify potential areas of conflict in your own marriage:

1. Do you know your spouse's favorite food, color, or hobby?
2. Do you know how much privacy your spouse needs or desires?
3. Do you know how many children your spouse would like?
4. Do you know your spouse's method for disciplining children?

5. Do you know your spouse's low point each day—that time when he or she is most vulnerable?
6. Do you know and respect your spouse's fears?
7. Do you know and respect your spouse's critical issues?
8. Do you know and respect your spouse's true feelings about your friends?
9. Do you know and respect your spouse's attitudes about family finances?
10. Do you know and respect your spouse's views/attitudes on sexual foreplay and intercourse?
11. Are you aware of insurance costs, mortgage payments, and utility rate increases?
12. Are you aware of what is involved in completing your family's tax return?
13. Are you aware of your spouse's professional desires and disappointments?
14. Are you aware of your spouse's greatest concern for your children?
15. Are you aware of your spouse's view of success?

Hopefully these questions will cause you to think of other questions that are more specific to your relationship. The more you understand (not necessarily accept) the views and attitudes of your spouse, the less likely you are to experience confrontation; on any journey, it is the unexpected bump in the road that does the most damage.

From Bridal Showers to Baby Showers— Childbearing and Children

Raising children is the most serious potential conflict we will discuss. Couples need to be honest with each other when it comes to bringing a new life into the world. Some people have children because "that's what married couples do." Others have children because the marital relationship is lacking and one or both spouses erroneously believes that a child will help reunite the couple. In this situation, the child becomes responsible for the welfare of the marriage, a role no child could or should be expected to fill. If a child comes into the world *to fill any type of need* for the parents, he or she becomes the kingpin around which the marriage survives. If the kingpin is struck down, the union has nothing on which to frame itself and it dissolves. Children are not pawns for adult use; they are individuals with lives and futures that are dependent, mostly in their early years, upon parents who are willing and able to sacrifice time and energy for the children's welfare! To bring children into an unhealthy relationship is nothing more than a recipe for conflict and abuse.

Hopefully before pregnancy, but definitely before the birth of the first child, expectant parents need to openly discuss and listen to each other's expectations about the rearing of this precious life. They need to determine what type of extracurricular activities they are willing to support. They need to know how each other feels about different sports or what musical instruments or training they want to include in their children's early years. It is important to understand the different educational opportunities available to children today: home-school, private, and public. Couples who fail to discuss these issues prior to having children may find themselves amazed when they reach the critical time of decision at just how different their individual preferences are. Awareness of these disagreements may occur so late that their children miss out on opportunities simply because the parents did not take the time to develop a consensus.

Bringing Home the Bacon—The Breadwinner Syndrome

What does a couple think about earning money? Do both want to work outside the home? Where does the care of children fit in with career goals? Too often we assume that we know what our spouses think about income and career. Sometimes a husband is willing to earn less money and care for the children so his wife can pursue an opportunity that is better for the family. A wife may not want to earn an income because she thinks her husband wants her to spend all of her energy raising the family and caring for the home. Often a wife does not want to work outside the home, but cultural pressure leads her to pursue a career for which she has little interest.

How a family obtains income is its own business. Our concern is that couples communicate openly about their professional dreams and desires. Whatever you decide as a couple, you must not sacrifice your children for your careers. If both partners want professional careers, that's fine as long as children do not become secondary to those pursuits. Women who struggle with their desire to rear children and also have a career should consider the possibility of nurturing their children through the toddler years while pursuing careers from within the home. For some, a twenty-year career is well within reach even if it is begun after the children's school years.[1] Brief, honest, and open discussion can do much to avoid unnecessary conflict by diminishing stereotypes and revealing concealed expectations that tend to change or develop as we and our children age.

"It's Only Money, But . . ."—Family Finances

People have different financial goals. During courtship, some couples tend to be more free in their spending habits as they try to impress a potential mate. Once the vows are completed, one spouse may become the proverbial tight-fisted miser while the other spouse continues to buy as if there were no tomorrow. Where a couple sits on this continuum is critical to marital bliss. All of us would find it extremely beneficial to develop a line-item budget prior to marriage and continue maintaining one throughout our journeys together. Financial expectations and views on credit cards, checking accounts, saving accounts, mutual funds, life insurance (term or whole-life), and retirement accounts should be discussed in order to discover each other's views on finances. One of the primary causes of marital conflict is finances. The experience we gain through bankruptcy may provide incentive for developing sound financial skills, but it is wiser and cheaper to develop such skills before bankruptcy occurs and without lawyers. We need to agree on financial strategies early in the marriage marathon and adjust our spending to our incomes.

"Cleanliness Is Next to . . ."—Organization and Chaos

Some people are simply more organized than others. Often a "Disaster Dan" marries a "Precision Pat." When this happens, all kinds of human expression is possible. Agreements need to be reached when differences in organization exist. One spouse wants the clothes placed neatly in the dresser while the other sees no reason to neatly organize something that is used on a regular basis. One spouse wants the checks registered when they are written at the store and the other prefers to wait until he or she sits down at the family's monthly budget meeting. One spouse sees the living-room floor as a gathering place for items that can be put away on the weekend, while the other spouse prefers that everything be put in its proper place at the end of each day. Differences along this continuum can lead to conflicts ad infinitum if we don't establish acceptable ground rules early in our marriages.

"How Do You Say . . . ?"—Communication

Some of us just have a kinship with words; they never stop coming out of our mouths. Though it is not necessary to change every interesting idiosyncrasy that we may have, it is important that arrangements be established that allow a less communicative spouse the opportunity to talk. Those of us who love to talk may not always be aware that our spouses are uncomfortable with the constant barrage of words. If you never express your frustration with the verbal blitz, your spouse will simply continue on as normal, thinking nothing of it. Communication is the channel through which *each spouse* reveals who he or she is. Never is the "shutdown" of a spouse good for a marriage. Those of us who are talkative don't need to change personalities; we need to be sensitive to our spouses' need to communicate, too, and ensure that we provide opportunities for that communication every day. Those of us who are reticent to speak do not need to learn to be the talkers of the town, either; we simply need to make our concerns, expectations, and opinions known so that we don't stifle our marriage relationships.

Today, Tomorrow, or Whenever—Timeliness

"Punctual Pete" marries "Whistle-Away Wendy" and realizes that he will never again know what it means to be on time. Will "Whistle-Away Wendy" recognize her husband's concern over lateness and adjust so that she arrives on time? It's not wise to mold your spouse to your own perspective. Not only is it impossible, it often brings undesirable conflict. We can learn to adjust to each other through collaboration. "Punctual Pete" almost always believes that punctuality is essential to his self-esteem and worth. "Whistle-Away Wendy" may consider lateness a status symbol, stylish, or an unavoidable reality of life: "After all, nothing really starts on time anyway." These two can buy separate vehicles, or they can agree on putting in extra effort to be on time for events they deem critical and to relax for events that are not time critical. With this potential conflict, as with all conflicts, you need to develop a sense of humor and learn to enjoy the uniqueness of the person you love and married. It's this, or have a cardiac arrest at age forty!

Enjoying Each Other—Sexuality

The person with the most testosterone (most often the male, but not always) seldom wins, especially if he marries "Nocturnal Nel," which often seems to be the case. Each couple has their own sexual comfort zone. No movie, magazine, or sex therapist can tell a couple what should be sexually comfortable. If your spouse is uncomfortable with a particular sex act, you shouldn't push the issue unless your spouse expresses a willingness to try. The problem with pornography is that it suggests behavior that often degrades women. It also turns women into instruments or toys for sexual pleasure. You must discover and learn to enjoy the comfort zone that your marriage and individual histories allow. To love your spouse is to honor him or her where he or she is truly the most vulnerable.[2]

The "Tempestuous-T Trilogy"—Household Comforts

The "Tempestuous-T Trilogy" represents all those little things a spouse does that drives the other absolutely crazy: Toothpaste, Temperature, and Toilet paper. It refers to the husband who picks nose hair in the theater, the wife who always forgets to shut the car door before she comes in the house, the husband who loses his wallet regularly, the wife who wonders every morning which lipstick looks best. These are those annoying things that actually give our spouses uniqueness and character. They keep a marriage from being static. They become the things that endear spouses to one another—or at least they should. To attempt to correct all these "little treasures" will wound a marriage. People are imperfect. In areas that have little significance in the big scope of things, spouses need to "take a chill pill." Maybe a wife can buy her husband nose hair clippers; a husband can learn to expect the car door to be left open and be sure to check it before going in for the evening or perhaps encourage his wife to bring the car into the garage (she'll probably leave the garage door open); a wife can help her husband find his wallet; and a husband can seize the opportunity each morning to comment on the attractiveness of his wife.

Any Violation of Trust

Any act that one spouse views as a violation of trust should be avoided. Trust takes too long to build and is too easy to lose. If your spouse is uncomfortable with one of your friendships, the relationship with the friend may have to be curtailed. The marriage relationship is more important than all others and should never be knowingly placed in jeopardy. It is inappropriate to suggest that your spouse should "get used to it." People grow in an environment that is safe and loving. You may think that your partner is overreacting, and he or she may in fact be; however, the protection of the union and the welfare and growth of your spouse supersedes all other concerns. At times, protecting your spouse's trust in you may appear to slow down the progress of the marriage marathon. But it never does. Marriage brings two people into a union that has never existed before in human history. Because each partner brings his or her own unique experiences into the union, no time-line for building trust can be established. Remember that you are not racing against anyone else and no one else is allowed to ride with you. You are traveling on a bicycle built for two individuals who must work in tandem to get the most from the journey. If you don't trust each other, suspicion will take over, communication will become defensive, and road blocks will pop up all along the way.[3]

Keeping the Peace

There are many activities you can embrace that protect your marriage from insensitive remarks, unintentional insults, and unnecessary harm. Though it is important to identify potential conflicts, it is equally important to develop guidelines that keep the peace on a daily basis. Since these guidelines are basically self-explanatory, they are listed for consideration and personal application.

1. Honor your spouse's opinions—spouses who are led to believe that their opinions are inconsequential eventually stop sharing them.
2. Think positive thoughts about your spouse—no matter what the circumstances, discipline yourself to think of your spouse with kind and gentle words.
3. Recognize your spouse's commitment and priorities—take time to discover them. Often the use of a calendar goes a long way toward keeping each other's commitments in mind.
4. Discuss one issue at a time—don't allow one issue to escalate into other related or unrelated issues that eventually leave you unaware of where the discussion began.
5. Be considerate and forgiving of your spouse's family. The reason society develops so many in-law jokes is because in-laws are an imperfect group. No matter how difficult your spouse's parents may be, or seem to be, it is most likely that your spouse retains

a loyalty to them and, therefore, hopes that "things" eventually will improve. Often the tension that comes from a difficult child/parent relationship does not destroy the child's love for his or her parents, or at least the desire for a renewed love. *If at all possible,* let any criticism of your in-laws come from your spouse while you lend an understanding ear and helpful advice when the time is appropriate. If you need to share a concern, do so, but share it calmly and respectfully. Control the anger and harsh words that may be lingering on the tip of your tongue. Remember that you are sharing your concerns with a teammate and, more importantly, with your best friend (see Romans 12:9–18 and James 3:1–12).

6. Work on issues corporately; don't condescend—marriage is a union designed to include the input of two equal persons who are willing to submit to one another. Treating a spouse as a subordinate is humiliating and counterproductive, and abuses a valuable resource.

7. Control your emotions when your spouse is frustrated or angry—to become a player in a volatile exchange just extends the "hurting zone." Even when the assault is directed at you, patience and understanding will help bring the intensity of the attack to an eventual calm and also allow your spouse to apologize more easily.

8. Be your spouse's number-one fan—everyone should have the privilege of trying something new and have the support of at least one fanatic person.

9. Remember the promises you make—if you don't think you will be able to keep a promise, don't make it. This is an area where trust is put in jeopardy.

10. Pay close attention to your spouse's efforts and express appreciation regularly—often we become so caught up in our own efforts or become so used to the efforts of our spouses that we forget to express gratitude and appreciation. "Thank you" is an expression that never loses its value.

11. Offer public recognition and never criticize in public—public praise of your spouse is a sure way to send a message to others that you value your relationship.

12. Control your thought (fantasy) life—to allow your mind to stray to "greener pastures" invades the privacy of others and is

tantamount to emotional adultery. In a world that has no lack of pornography from adult bookstores to on-line live-action photography, our world does all it can to destroy the most important human relationship you can have. Avoid pornography and don't underestimate its devastating consequences. The only nude person you want to visualize is the spouse who has promised to love you intimately for life. Treasure that relationship in body and in mind!

Photographing Your Relationship: An Evaluation Tool

One tool designed to help couples periodically evaluate the quality of their relationship is called *photographing*. At the end of each day or week, sit down with your spouse before bedtime to evaluate the quality of your marriage. Take a mental photograph or video of your relationship through a given period (a day, a week, but no more than two weeks). With number one being low quality and number ten being high, rate each other's performance. You are *not* permitted to argue with your spouse's scoring or defend your actions. If your spouse gives you a six, discuss what took place that caused the loss of four points. Accept your spouse's explanation and make the necessary adjustments to improve your score at a later evaluation. Then discuss what you did that was appreciated and earned a score of six. The roles are then reversed and the same procedure is followed. It is important that you each start discussing the negative and end by discussing the positive. As you lie down to sleep next to your spouse, your relationship begins fresh with a score of ten. This procedure helps to get the negative things settled and the positive things accentuated so that evil, in the form of unresolved conflict, does not gain an advantage in the relationship (see Eph. 4:25–32).

This tool is extremely conducive to helping you discuss thoughts and feelings safely with your spouse, informing each other of shortcomings and achievements in a peaceful setting, diminishing your natural tendency to defend yourself, and putting disappointments behind you more quickly. The skill gives you the opportunity to practice all the strategy statements. It is a positive skill that allows every evaluation period to begin and end with a grade of *A*.

Conflict Squelchers

Conflicts are inevitable, but they do not have to escalate. There are ways to cool down a heated exchange with your marriage partner. Each of these procedures allows you to regain your composure so that you can find resolution through merging each other's differing perspectives. Often when arguing with your spouse, you need to take a time-out for fifteen to sixty minutes. Too much heat leads to combustion, especially when you keep adding fuel. The time-out should not exceed sixty minutes because either you or your spouse may forget some of the key details or simply become too removed from the discussion to want to continue it. The time-out is not a time to plan strategy for defeating your spouse's position. It is a time of reflection and collection in which you prepare yourself to mentally and emotionally reenter the discussion with the best interests of your spouse in mind.

Upon returning to the discussion, it is imperative that both you and your spouse commit to remaining seated and to speaking in low voices. Standing during a conflict symbolizes control, and a loud voice suggests dominance. Both are a hindrance to productive communication. You should attempt to sit across from your spouse so that you can see into each other's eyes. The eyes are a great reflector of the heart. The more you can look into each other's eyes, the more peace is achieved. It is difficult to look into the eyes of a person with whom there is no unity or bond.

While discussing a difficult issue, there is no excuse for spouse-bashing. Regurgitating previous failures, calling each other names, and mocking proposed solutions do nothing to resolve conflict. The purpose of a discussion is to seek a mutual solution, not to force agendas. If you lose respect for each other, you have no past on which to build a future. Using words and attitudes that belittle and degrade will destroy the good you've done in your marriage. A refrigerator magnet bears the message, "Kids may forget what you said, but they will never forget how you made them feel." This saying is equally true of spouses.

Tone or body language that reflects a lack of care or an aura of supremacy makes your spouse unwilling to participate in what is obviously a one-sided conversation. Openness is lost along with the trust and intimacy that follow from it. Your tone and body language need to project an attitude of concern and a desire to seek mutual resolution. We communicate and find resolution more quickly in an environment that accepts differing opinions.

Listening is difficult primarily because it involves placing your own agenda on the shelf in order to saturate yourself with the thoughts, feelings, and desires of your spouse. Listening is a choice that has its roots in love. It longs to understand so that it can meet needs thoroughly.

Stay on the topic. Arguments between spouses are infamous for covering every issue that has brought discomfort over the past decade. This technique hurts the relationship and does nothing to bring resolution. Resolution is difficult enough when dealing with only one issue; it is totally impossible when the issues multiply.

Finally you must avoid the temptation to interrupt your spouse or to correct him or her unless the error is blatant. Interruption shows a lack of interest in understanding a spouse's perspective and is defensive. If corrections must be made, relate them to a statement that is central to the discussion. Minor corrections about the time of day or the color of a shirt usually are irrelevant and should be overlooked to ensure that the conversation stays focused on the topic.

Summary and Strategy Progression

Conflict is an opportunity that challenges every couple to run from selfish individualism and to develop a oneness or union. It dares us to discover the potential that can be realized when we fully join resources with our spouses. When we marry, we must find solutions that are best for the couple rather than for one individual. Conflict reminds us of the need to remain committed to principles that protect and promote the value of marriage.[4]

Each of the preceding strategies creates a mind-set that makes pursuing growth during conflict a real possibility. Without a commitment to the welfare of your spouse based on an unconditional love that allows vulnerability and honesty in communication, you will not have the wherewithal to commit to resolving conflict, much less establish goals that are realistic and timely. Note again how each strategy builds toward the next and that each strategy is dependent on the strategy that precedes it.

The next section challenges us to keep our marriages adventurous and satisfying by setting mutual goals. In the same way that cyclists set fitness goals through an exercise regimen, timing goals to improve speed, and financial goals to acquire the best equipment in order to give them the rides of their lives, so we must set goals for our marriages in order to gain a sense of purpose and direction.

"I will place my spouse's needs before my own."

"I will daily love, honor, and encourage my spouse."

"I will practice a style of communication that allows my spouse to be vulnerable and honest at all times."

"I will seek resolution and growth during conflict."

You have just passed Marriage Marathon Milestone 4. Keep peddling!

❧ Strategy Five ❧

*I will set timely and realistic
goals with my spouse.*

Goal-Setting: Planning Timely and Realistic Goals Together

What will your marriage look like next year? What about in five years or fifteen years? When we get married, we have expectations about a life filled with joy and opportunity. Some of our expectations are known to our spouses, but often they are not. We assume that our love for each other as well as our common interests will take us in the same direction. It appears, however, that many couples riding the same bicycle are going in different directions; couples seldom schedule time together to develop and set mutual goals. It's surprising to learn that somewhere in the neighborhood of only 3 percent of married couples set realistic and timely goals for their marriage.[1]

Life as a couple is more than staying married, buying a car and a home, bringing some children into the world, and hopefully reaching a ripe old age with as few medical inconveniences as possible. Those of us whose lives are shortsighted ultimately find ourselves controlled by the events of life that unfold before us. Eventually we spin out of control. All the joys and expectations with which we began our journeys together run into dead ends created by an agenda left to chance.

If a marriage relationship is to progress and remain vital, it needs daily direction, purpose, and reward. We need to awake each day, knowing that our day's efforts hold significance. Expending energy for no other purpose than paying the bills is futile and reveals an attitude inconsistent with commitments of love and concern for the welfare and growth of our spouses. Marriage provides the opportunity to pursue the challenges of life as a team with dual resources: two minds, two hearts, and two bodies funneled into a single purpose—establishing and meeting goals that ensure the welfare and growth of the union.

When couples view marriage as a lifelong commitment, they need to establish long-range goals. The minds, spirits, and bodies of each spouse should work together to develop a union capable of physically and emotionally sheltering and feeding one another, of providing and caring for the children it may produce, of establishing and maintaining the career(s) that furnishes its financial base, of encouraging and developing special interests that give the union an occasional and needed burst of energy, and of ensuring peace and security when the marriage marathon reaches its later years. From the starting point to the finish line, goals are necessary to develop such a union. Without set goals, couples allow circumstances and emotions to turn their journeys through life into a safari with unsuspected danger at every turn. Threat in a marriage has a way of taking joy and opportunity out of it. What began with enviable enthusiasm, dies in a cloud of confusion. Goals, however, blow the clouds away and blaze a trail through a jungle of challenges. Daily loving, honoring, and encouraging our spouses develops communications skills and styles that make the creation of goals and the commitment to fulfill them an actual reality in marriage. Goals provide a tremendous tool through which we meet our spouses' needs.

Direction identifies the path that is to be pursued. As you and your spouse agree upon a path that leads to a specific destination, your daily efforts gain purpose and meaning. As the directions are followed and destinations are reached, you are rewarded. You believe you are important to each other when mutual effort is expended for the benefit of your marriage. Completing goals builds greater trust and intimacy.

The purpose of this section is to describe the importance of goals;

to encourage you to disclose your individual expectations to your spouse; to explain how to set goals that are specific, realistic, timely, and have impact; and to provide a tool through which personal and mutual goals can be established and reached.

Marriage Strategy 5

The strategy that brings goals to completion reflects your willingness to practice the principles that accompany the preceding four strategy statements. Mutual goals will not exist in relationships that are self-serving. Only a love that places the welfare of your spouse above your own can create an environment of healthy communication through which goals can be formulated. And only goals that are realistic and time sensitive have the opportunity of being reached. Therefore, each of you must add to your overall marriage marathon strategy a commitment that works toward the formation of quality goals: *"I will set timely and realistic goals with my spouse."*

CHAPTER 16

Marriage's Mirages: The Problem with Goal-Setting

*W*hen we assume that our dreams and plans are possible without the assistance of others or think that others will naturally understand and follow along, the pictures of success we see in our minds are only mirages waiting to vanish before eyes opened to reality. Herein lies the primary problem that causes a couple to neglect goal-setting: they believe that good things will happen in their marriage when neither spouse knows what the other thinks is good or proper. The course taken and the speed with which that course is covered must be decided upon together with a complete understanding of each other's expectations.

Examining Each Other's Expectations

Expectations play a powerful role in the failure or the success of a marriage. If you aren't familiar with the hopes and dreams of your spouse, you cannot focus your attention on establishing goals that take your spouse's hopes and dreams into consideration. Ultimately your partner will become frustrated with your apparent unwillingness to consider his or her needs and desires in your plans. Often your spouse is *expecting* your participation in meeting his or her desires without letting you know what those desires are.

A couple who develop expectations for one another without letting each other know about those expectations becomes discouraged and eventually isolated from one another. While one partner gets discouraged, the other gets confused. When we take time to discuss important issues with our spouses and listen to their wants and desires, we then are able to use this information to develop personal and marital goals. Consequently, our spouses feel appreciated and become valued participants in our personal lives as well as in our marriages. Your expectations of your spouse should be based on *shared information* rather than private information. When you know your expectations of one another, they have a greater chance of being realized. With this in mind, it is necessary that we define *expectations*.

A Definition of Expectation

Expectation is the act of thinking that something is coming or is going to take place. It implies that we are anticipating or looking for a particular event *usually* in a hopeful, rather than regretful manner. An expectation is most often a hope for future good or profit, like a good harvest or productive relationship. An expectation is neither good nor bad in and of itself, unless the person on whom the expectation rests knows nothing about it.

Sources of Expectation

Some suggest that there are two basic causes for trouble in marriage: first, not finding in marriage what you expected, and second, not expecting what you actually find! The experiences you have before getting married create hopes and dreams that are often different from those created by the person with whom you fall in love and marry. Each of you, thinking you have found the person who can fulfill your youthful expectations, too frequently and naively assume your partner has similar expectations and will live in a manner consistent with them. As time passes and expectations are left unfulfilled, conflict ensues or your spouse, in an attempt to avoid conflict, suppresses his or her disappointment. Either way, the marriage is in trouble.

Expectations, whether established before or during marriage, are powerful and need to be clearly disclosed to each partner. It is imperative to remember that some expectations are not clearly understood by the person who possesses them until an event reveals the expectation. For example, a wife reacts coldly to her husband, who took their two young children to the beach to swim in the surf. The husband, a qualified lifesaver, assures his wife that he kept the children within reach at all times; nevertheless, the wife remains agitated. Surprised by her own reaction, she pauses to evaluate the cause of her agitation.

She discovers that she expected her husband to have the same fear of the sea that she does. Her knowledge of the ocean came from movies and novels that spoke of the terror of the sea. She grew up in the Mid-west, while he grew up on the California coast. Her previous swimming activities had always been near a pool, where she apparently felt safe. But swimming in the ocean produced a reaction for which neither the woman nor her husband was prepared. Coming to understand her ex-pectation allowed this couple to develop a swimming plan for the chil-dren that was acceptable to both spouses.

Life-shaping experiences create our dreams and methods for han-dling situations. A young boy may watch an old movie that depicts a wife thoroughly devoted to her husband and his career. The movie satisfies a particular longing, and the boy establishes an expectation about the woman he is going to marry before he even knows her name. A young girl watches a television show about a woman whose hus-band is always gone, is disrespectful to her, and lacks any type of com-mitment to her professional welfare. She is affected so negatively by the show that she creates an expectation about her future husband that does not allow for extended absences, and that demands that he be 100 percent supportive of her desire to pursue a legal education.

You may have been impressed by the relationship of a couple you respect, and have decided to emulate that relationship in your own marriage. Or you may have seen negative qualities in someone's rela-tionship and determined that those qualities can never be a part of your marriage marathon. People listen to different kinds of music, have theological and various shades of traditional upbringing, and receive counseling either personally or through educational means. All these experiences define the way they think marriage is *supposed* to be. If one of your "supposed to be's," is an expectation not known to your spouse, it is unlikely that it will ever be addressed and fulfilled. When this happens, disappointment is inevitable.

Examples of Faulty Expectations

Many people have expectations about marriage that are based in hope rather than reality. Like an apparent oasis in the desert, their expectations are mirages that time will eventually erase. If they can-not adjust, their marriage marathons will dry up in the blustering and unforgiving winds of reality.

Faulty expectations are numerous. Some of us marry, believing that the feelings we had during courtship will always remain. We falsely assume that we will never experience feelings of doubt about the spouses we chose to marry. Others believe that they have found spouses with whom they will never argue, or they marry spouses whom they know have some different tastes and opinions, but they are convinced that eventually these tastes and opinions will change. Maybe your spouse has developed an annoying habit, but you think your spouse is as concerned about it as you and will overcome it.

Some of us expect our children to have characteristics that will remain consistent with our own. Others of us actually believe that our in-laws will never interfere with our marriages or the raising of our children. A few of us have the unrealistic opinion that our love for one another will overcome the absence of money. Some of us strongly maintain that nothing will prevent us from caring for our aging parents or that we will ever have to. Divorced persons erroneously believe that a second attempt at marriage will be easier because we are less likely to make the same mistakes.

Though we may long to reach these marriage mirages, we can't be dogmatic about the possibility of them actually being within reach. Though some of us may be able to care for our parents, circumstances may prevent others from doing so. Once in a while two people marry who never have a harsh word to say to one another, but this is quite rare, and it's unwise to expect this as a norm for marriage. We may hope for the perfect ride, but we are wise if we prepare for a marriage that contains random acts of imperfection.

Unrealistic expectations create unrealistic goals. If a rural fellow expects his fiancée from the city to eventually appreciate and occasionally accompany him on his hunting trips, he would be wise to inform her of this hope and set realistic goals that allow her to slowly acclimate to a more outdoor type of lifestyle. Goals built on unrealistic expectations have little hope of succeeding. Rather than bringing unity, they promote isolation.

The Arc of Expectation

It sounds like geometry, but it's really about marriage. The arc of expectation evaluates the difference between reality and our expectations. If our expectations are unknown or unrealistic, a greater gap exists between what we expect should happen and what actually happens. In marriage, the wider the gap, the greater dissatisfaction and frustration we experience. The more our expectations line up with reality, the greater our satisfaction in the marriage and the more plausible our goals. Expectations that are disclosed to each other and that are realistic (attainable) create realistic goals that are designed to fulfill expectations.

If a wife expects her husband to make some friendships that can provide enjoyment for both of them, she must first disclose this desire. After the disclosure, the couple can realistically create a goal that brings friends into the relationship that the two of them can enjoy together. If a husband expects his wife to financially and emotionally support the relationship at the same level she did before the birth of their children, the gap that is created between his expectation and reality will bring frustration and despair to the relationship. This expectation is unrealistic, and any goals connected to this expectation are equally unrealistic.

Eventually, we will be confronted by expectations that we didn't even know we had. These unacknowledged expectations often bring discord. You need to regularly identify and evaluate both your own and your spouse's expectations to ensure that you both find them agreeable. You cannot commit to something of which you or your spouse are unaware or with which you disagree. Only as you remain aware of your spouse's hopes and desires—his or her expectations—can your marriage develop toward sensitive or practical oneness. *Undeclared personal expectations lead to an unfulfilled marriage experience.* If you let your spouse know where you want to go, it is easier to prepare a plan that ensures that he or she will be there, physically and emotionally, when you arrive.

CHAPTER 17

Marriage's Little Markers: The Purpose and Process of Goal-Setting

I don't think this is going anywhere!" Have you ever been in a long race or been involved in a project that takes days or weeks to accomplish? To avoid boredom, weariness, or a sense of futility, we take the big event (goal) and chop it up into a bunch of little events (goals). Think about the grueling reality of completing a one hundred-mile bicycle marathon (for a noncyclist, the thought is overwhelming). If finishing is your only goal, twenty miles down the road you'll end up thoroughly drained and beaten by the course. But if you set dietary goals, workout goals, and break up the race into five twenty-mile races with individual goals for each segment, not only will you have a better chance of completing the race in your best time ever, but you will also find the total experience chock-full of victories and rewards. Little encouragements along the way make the completion of any journey more thrilling.

Here's another example. Do you remember the first day of the school year? In each class, the instructor lays out the strategy for the whole semester along with an exhaustive list of student requirements. At the end of the day, the possibility of completing all that homework appears impossible. To see all that work as an undivided whole is like seeing an avalanche falling down on you with no place to go; a cold, oxygen-free death is all that awaits you. But in time, you settle your emotions and begin the process of breaking down your work class by class and week by week. Soon the big load is broken down into manageable little loads, all placed in a schedule that makes the journey through them seem possible. Each assignment finished builds to the ultimate completion of the semester.

Every long-term goal, whether it's completing the marriage marathon or buying a new bicycle, cries out for short-term goals to make the process palatable and purposeful. We need little markers along the way as we journey forward toward our ultimate mark. The goal or mark of every couple is to successfully complete the marriage marathon; little goals or markers are developed to keep couples focused and fulfilled along the way.

Balancing Personal and Relational Goals

Relational goals in marriage spring from the personal goals that each spouse establishes. Without personal direction, there is little chance for relational direction. Constructive relational or marital goals must involve some degree of correlation with each spouse's personal goals if you hope to be involved with and supportive of your spouse. Though some personal goals may not directly involve your partner, other than through encouragement, most personal goals need to be blended together to create relational or mutual goals. The pursuit of these relational goals gives direction and purpose to the marriage, mutual satisfaction, and ultimately freedom to achieve some independent personal goals. Husbands and wives are much more willing to support the personal goals of each other if they are convinced that the relational goals take precedence.

Characteristics of Effective Goal-Setting

In order for any goal to be productive, it must be clearly identified through the use of at least four characteristics. The *first* characteristic requires that the goal be *specific*. This first characteristic has two steps, the first of which is to determine a category in which we want to work. Are we looking for an intellectual challenge, physical fitness, emotional stability, spiritual growth, social interaction, educational advancement, financial improvement, family unity, or professional development? After identifying a specific category, the second step to making a goal specific involves asking five open-ended questions:

1. What specifically in the identified category do I want to accomplish?
2. Where do I have to go to accomplish it?

3. Who else is involved in bringing the goal to fruition?
4. Why is this issue or objective important enough to pursue?
5. How do I reach the objective or goal?

These questions force answers that keep your goal from becoming vague or unclear. The clearer the goal, the more dedicated the effort to complete it! Suppose a wife suggests to her husband that she would like to find a different job that would give her more freedom. She has identified the category as professional. A quick run through the questions in the second step will identify the procedures necessary to pursue this goal. What is it she would like to accomplish? She responds, "A job that would let me be my own boss." Where would you like to work? "Preferably in my home, as in a home business." Who would be involved with the business? At this point, a specific business can be identified, as well as the people she would need to contact to begin that business. Why do you want to begin a home business? "I want to make my own hours and see if I have the ability to run a business on my own." How will you reach the objective? Here, specific responsibilities and procedures are identified that make the beginning of the business possible. To be more specific, the couple will continue to ask open-ended questions until the goal is clearly identified and a procedure for reaching the goal has been developed.

The *second* characteristic demands that the specific goal is *realistic*. Do you believe your goal is reachable given the personal resources and skills you have? If the answer is no, you must adjust the goal to a more realistic level. Often people try to take on more than they are able to handle. This eventually leads to discouragement and the loss of desire to pursue what might have been a potentially good goal. If this happens too often, people generally give up trying to achieve goals. You must attempt what you are presently able to handle. Accomplishing something small can lead to other opportunities of which you aren't even aware. Be realistic!

Third, goals need to have a *time limit*. When is the goal going to be pursued and how much time can you devote to it? Does it require a daily, weekly, or monthly block of time? If you fail to set time limits, goals tend to get ignored. Our natural tendency toward procrastination is overcome by a schedule. Create a time line to which you can commit, and stick to it. Without a time limit, goals get lost in the twilight zone!

The *fourth* characteristic that is essential to good goal-setting concerns itself with the *impact* the goal has on you, your family and friends, and others. In a society that encourages individualism, how our actions impact others is a low priority. Life is intended, however, to be lived in a social context that requires personal responsibility. Everything we do impacts someone, so it is critical that we consider how our goals will impact others. In asking yourself about the impact of your goals, you force yourself to consider whether this goal will have negative or positive influences on everyone it touches. If you discover that a goal may negatively affect a family member, friend, or neighbor, some adjustments can be made to avoid the difficulty by refocusing an aspect of the goal. How a goal affects you, your partner, your children, and others often determines the level of commitment you place on pursuing the goal and the level of stress that accompanies it.

A Method for Effective Goal-Setting

The purpose of the Goal Wheel is to develop an easy system through which couples can identify specific, realistic, timely, and impact-oriented goals. The "HUSBAND" and "WIFE" goal wheels on pages 171–72 are designed to give you the opportunity to develop eight personal goals in eight distinct categories. Personal goal wheels should be filled out individually—one by the husband and one by the wife. This allows you to declare wants and desires without being influenced by your spouse, although you shouldn't ignore how a goal might impact your spouse.

It's critical that you select a goal in each category. Like water, we find our natural levels. If we aren't required to place a goal in each category, we will naturally migrate to those categories in which it is easier for us to work. Often the category we find most difficult is the area in which we most need to set goals. Work in this area may have the most lasting impact on our lives.

The outside circle is provided to place the main or long-term goal in each category. The inside circle focuses on the steps or short-term goals that need to be accomplished en route to the long-term goal.

After you complete your personal goal wheel and your spouse completes his or her wheel, compare wheels so that the two of you can develop suitable goals for your marriage. A "COUPLE" goal wheel (bottom of page 172) is used in this process. From your personal wheels, develop goals in each category that you would like to accept as relational or mutual goals. For every category, you will have two sets of goals to compare. Therefore, compare wheels to see if the two of you desire similar goals. Where agreement exists, a relational goal is immediately established in that category. Where there are dissimilarities, choose one of the suggested goals and pursue it relationally, or jointly develop a different relational goal in that category. As you work together through a category where dissimilarities exist, keep in mind the four strategies that we have discussed so far. If you remembered, while writing your personal goals, to consider the impact or the effect your goals would have on your spouse, then the first strategy has already been at work in your heart and, therefore, you are well prepared to develop mutual goals with your spouse. As you move through each category together, honor and encourage one another by giving each other time to discuss the purpose and importance of personal goals. Being sensitive to your spouse's needs will help you to listen more intently and be more open to permanently or temporarily doing away with a dissimilar goal, or adjusting it to work more in line with your spouse's goal. Remain open to new ways of doing things, and keep the discussion friendly and safe. Goal-setting is not a contest of wills and ideas; rather, it is a collaborative effort designed to help the two of you keep to the same course or direction.

GOAL WHEELS

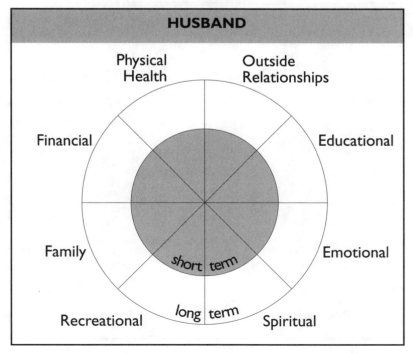

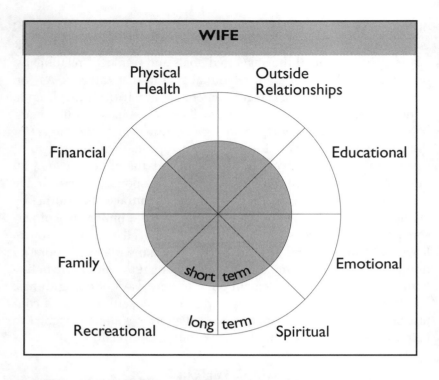

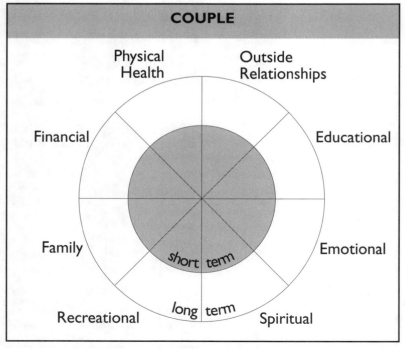

At the end of this exercise, each spouse has a set of personal and relational long-term goals with short-term steps for bringing them to reality. Another benefit is the insight you both gain into each other's hopes and expectations; you stay aware of what is important to one another and become supporters and players in accomplishing each other's dreams. Today is always brighter when tomorrow's path is lined with lights. Know where you're going so that what you do today has purpose.

Summary and Strategy Progression

Goals cannot be developed freely in an environment that doesn't follow the strategies outlined in the previous sections. To collaborate in the establishment of relational goals, you must be concerned with the welfare of your spouse. To understand and act in correlation with the hopes, dreams, and expectations of your spouse is to honor and respect him or her and is the reflection of an environment that encourages the free exchange of ideas. Collaboration in goal-setting is the product of good conflict resolution skills. It promotes stability in your marriage, develops greater trust, and opens the door to more intimate involvement with one another, which leads us to our final strategy. Healthy romance is the culmination of and reward for consistently living according to strategies 1 through 5 of the marriage marathon as well as adhering to some principles we will now look at that are specific to nurturing romance.

"I will place my spouse's needs before my own."

"I will daily love, honor, and encourage my spouse."

"I will practice a style of communication that allows my spouse to be vulnerable and honest at all times."

"I will seek resolution and growth during conflict."

"I will set timely and realistic goals with my spouse."

You have just passed Marriage Marathon Milestone 5. Keep peddling!

❧ Strategy Six ❧

*I will nurture romance
through daily care.*

Romance: Adding Zing
to the Journey

The dictionary defines romance as "adventure stories, poems, and stories of heroes, noble deeds, and the like" that are full of love and excitement.[1] The popular idea that romance is synonymous with sex is far from the truth. Romance involves zing, playfulness, courtship, honor, courage, chivalry, travel, and much more before it opens opportunity for the most intimate form of romance, sexual intercourse, or more accurately, the sexual union that encompasses the whole of the act.

Romance is an adventure that begins when a married couple's eyes first find each another in the courtship days and should last until the moment when the Lord calls one or both partners to His side. In marriage, romance is daily interaction that gives life together meaning, security, comfort, hope, peace, and fun. A romantic marriage is one that regularly pursues adventure and is based on the attributes of love, honor, respect, and encouragement. It is a story of two lovers, daily caring for the welfare of the other in a disruptive environment that challenges their unity and existence.

It is *not* an adventure that joins two youthful people in a riveting plot full of intrigue and danger, where they eventually overcome the immediate odds to live romantically and happily ever after. Romance is not as simple as a Disney fairy tale. A romantic marriage is a strategic, challenging, and exotic adventure that *overcomes the odds throughout a couple's lifetime.*[2]

Though romantic endeavors bring people together with surreptitious glances, hormonal impulses, and costumed courtships in which individuals strut their best stuff to lure a potential mate, romance cannot flourish and bring lasting satisfaction unless it finds its proper place in the marriage marathon. Romance is an adventure working in ever-expanding circles that are entirely dependent on the strategies and principles described in the preceding sections of this book. As a relationship develops, it learns more about itself. The desire to love deepens. As love grows, honor and encouragement become more pronounced. With honor grows a greater willingness to communicate more vulnerably. As communication becomes more vulnerable and spouse-centered, the relationship gains trust. As trust grows, confidence expresses itself, and intimacy or oneness moves from the positional actuality at the altar, to peaceful resolutions of conflict, and to practical expressions of unity in goal-setting.

Within this process, a romantic story is being written that continues to grow. No boundaries or ranges can be placed on the circles of romance. It is an adventure that grows in correlation to a couple's commitment to one another. *Romance is a reward that is won as the result of consistent effort and attention.* It is the zing that keeps participation in the marriage marathon exhilarating. Couples need to be reminded of the wonder of passion, of the romantic diversions they can choose to enhance their attraction to one another, and of the effort required to make romance possible. This section on romance seeks to motivate you to pursue *living out the strategies* that make the marriage marathon everything its Designer intended it to be.

Marriage Strategy 6

Because romance is worth pursuing and enhancing, a commitment is required that explicitly reminds each spouse of the effort that must be expended: *"I will nurture romance through daily care."* What begins with a simple look continues and matures only with daily care. Romance is more than kind words on a date, cuddling in front of the television, going shopping together, or being sexually intimate. Although these things are romantic, they do not represent all of what romance within marriage should be.

Romance can be making mutual efforts to maintain a home, defending a spouse who is misjudged, changing schedules to meet the needs of a spouse, admitting wrong and seeking forgiveness, or waiting for hours at the bedside of a spouse who has been seriously injured in an automobile accident. Romance happens when you commit yourself to meeting your spouse's *needs* (not necessarily wants) daily, no matter what you discover those needs to be.[3] Hugging, holding hands, cuddling on the couch, kissing, and sexual interplay are not mere duties. They are mutually desired romantic reactions that come as a result of selfless actions generated by a thoughtful, devoted, and caring friend and spouse. Romance is not an assumption, a guarantee, or an effortless expectation; it is a lifelong process, a worthy struggle, and a reward!

CHAPTER 18

Romance Happens When . . .

*R*omance happens when you make it happen. We'll admit that, at times, hormones stimulate romance without the need for strategies, principles, and the like; for romance to be a steady presence throughout the life of a relationship, however, *it must be intentional and based on daily care.* During our marriage retreats, we separate the men from the women and ask both groups to discuss what is romantic to men and then what is romantic to women. You'll read about some of the responses in the next few pages; others, well, they're better left to a retreat setting.

One thing is certain: men usually have more difficulty discussing what is romantic to women, except for the newlyweds and a few guys who overcame the initial conquering stage of marriage and replaced it with perpetual courtship. The women, on the other hand, fly through the exercise, usually doubling the men's output. Guys tend to place romance on hold, or better, simply forget that romance involves more than foreplay and intercourse until their wives, through a multitude of means, remind them of the necessity of continued courtship.

Romance happens when someone plans for it to happen; it may come as a surprise, but even surprises need to be planned. Spontaneous surprises are great too, but they often conflict with plans that the "surprised" spouse made that are unknown to the spouse planning the surprise. Try spontaneity from time to time, but don't rely on it. Planning is better! We know a wife who wanted to surprise her husband on Valentine's Day by appearing at the door wrapped in nothing but red crepe paper. A problem developed because her husband was not aware of her desire to surprise him. Seeing no need to rush home, he hung around the office to complete some extra work before heading home. Two hours after what she thought would be his arrival time, he came through the door and discovered his romantic surprise. She also got a Valentine's Day surprise—the moisture that developed on her warm, wrapped body merged with the red dye to leave a lasting impression. She dressed in long-sleeved, high-necked clothing for a few weeks until the red wore off. This is a wonderful idea, but along with the search for romantic zing, you have to be willing to suffer certain side-effects.

Remembering the Past: Romantic Memories

Those of you who have been married awhile, added a child or two to your busy lives, and spent the last few years focused on your careers need a moment to pause and reflect upon your romance escapades of the past, to those special occasions that make up your romantic memories. Do you remember what attracted you to your spouse? Was it her eyes, long hair, caring smile, or that straightforward and honest personality; his humor, confident aura, or thoughtfulness? Where did your first date take place, and what is your fondest memory of that occasion? Did he forget to bring enough money to pay the bill? Did she wear a dress that has forever been etched in the romantic museum of the mind? What was the most unforgettable experience that took place on your wedding day, or what was a highlight of your honeymoon? New memories are often fueled by the memory of old ones—those memories we fondly file in the category of better times. Lack of romance is synonymous with lack of attention. What are seen as better times need to become the impetus for what will be greater times.

What's Romantic to Men and Women?

While John was shopping for bedroom furniture with his wife, Shelly, a saleswoman made the comment that there could be nothing more romantic than a woman lying down beside her husband on their beautiful bed, surrounded by their gorgeous bedroom furniture, talking for an hour about their day's activities. Being a man, John was struck with an amusing thought about the romantic proposal the woman's husband might have been considering during that arduous hour. But as a woman, Shelly went for the atmosphere pitch, and they now own a rather expensive set of oak bedroom furniture. It is beautiful, but John reminds us that it doesn't compare to his wife!

Though much of what men and women desire in romance is similar, there are some basic differences. Men tend to be more visual and physical and emphasize respect as a critical romantic need, while women tend to desire more relational events and emphasize caring and validation as essential romantic needs. For women, romance happens when: (1) he kisses her gently on the lips and makes her feel as if he and she are the only two people in the room, (2) he gives her a bear hug when they first get out of bed, (3) he laughs with her about a story she shares, (4) he includes the family in his hobby, (5) he supports her career or business ventures, (6) he chases her around the house in his boxer shorts, (7) he buys her something that is comfortable rather than sexy, (8) he chooses her over the guys at the party, (9) he understands the discomforts of PMS, and (10) he shaves when he wants to fool around. Women enjoy gifts that have special symbolism. They appreciate actions that affirm that they are special. They want to feel vital and important, and they enjoy feeling protected and honored. Women love to be courted. They like to have their husbands initiate dating from time to time, and while they enjoy the sensual and physical side of romance, they see it as the grand finale or the fruit of daily care rather than the intent of daily care.

For men, romance happens when: (1) she gives him a hug every morning, (2) she compliments him for something he's done for her, (3) she gives him space when he needs it, (4) she meets him at the door in a fur coat with nothing on underneath, (5) she tells him he's a good father and husband, (6) she lights candles in the bedroom, (7) she puts love notes in his lunch, (8) she honors him in front of others, (9) she supports him in his decisions, and (10) she buys him tools. Men find their worth in being well respected. They tend to be guarded in their sentimentality and enjoy the sensual part of romance. Men like to receive gifts, and they love to be seen as their wives' champions. Men consider adventurous dates on a raft trip down the Colorado River exhilarating. However, relationally, the typical man is more fragile than he acts, and therefore he loves to be praised by the woman in his life.[1]

Couples need to take the time to ask one another what each considers romantic. It's also a good idea for each of you to graciously inform the other of what you think is not romantic. There are certain ways that both genders behave that do nothing to stimulate romance, for example, talking about work or the kids during foreplay, playing with nose hair or scraping out earwax while out for dinner, and wearing full-dress body armor to bed. This exercise will go far in eliminating any unrealistic or unknown expectations about what a spouse may or may not consider romantic. Unknown romantic needs remain unmet! Like so many other things in marriage, romance is built on good communication, not intuition!

CHAPTER 19

Romance Is for Everyone!

*T*he cycle of romance consists of three stages that revolve around the strategy statements discussed throughout this book: the "playful investigative" stage, the "personal commitment" stage, and the "mutual commitment" stage. As the cycle begins its first evolution, prior to marriage, the commitments are immature and unchallenged by time and experience. The cycle does not make its first complete circuit until a couple makes their commitment of marriage at the altar. At this point the cycle begins its second evolution of, it is hoped, a series of many more.

For most couples, romance's adventure begins with an extended stage during the teenage and young adult years in which two members of the opposite sex attempt to kick-start a lifelong relationship. It is a time of investigation, cautious vulnerability, wonder, childlike playfulness, flirtation, hope, and wounded hearts as individuals look for that special person with whom they can write a romantic story as they participate in the marriage marathon. During this period, people tend to hide their weaknesses because each wants to please and be exactly, or at least close to, what their pursuer desires. At the beginning of the cycle of romance, this stage tends to be more selfish, and change is motivated more by a desire to please than by personal commitment. Through trial and error, hopeful "intendeds" try to remember the likes and dislikes of their partners, dates and promises they make, and the advice they get from well-meaning families and friends who too often like the title of matchmaker. Some couples fail to make it through this stage and continue their search, some give up on the prospect of a romantic adventure, and some move on to the next stage, which invokes the idea of personal commitment.

During the second stage of the cycle of romance, couples marvel over the possibility of living out their lives together, talk of engagement, develop mutual interests and goals, and dream about the adventures and possibilities that might one day be written in their marriage autobiographies. Positive vibrations are generally flowing so smoothly that their love appears to be as strong as it could possibly get. Expectations that define the perfect marriage are often independently fashioned and appear as certainties. The "big question" seldom comes as a surprise but is welcomed with as much hoopla as the lift-off of a space shuttle. Yet underneath all the joy and apparent certainty quietly lingers the unthinkable notion that it may not all be bed and roses.

The third stage in the first evolution of the cycle of romance is the wedding period. Commitment moves from a personal to a mutual level. At this point the marriage has begun, and the care and respect, as well as the interest in and support of each other, create a thorough willingness to submit to one another in the most romantic expression of intimacy in which human beings can participate—sexual intercourse. Sexual intercourse or making love is a symbol of the mutual commitment that two people have for one another and for the children with whom they might be blessed. It is the *culmination of every caring action and comment* during the previous two courtship periods that resonates with the sounds of commitment. It is from these sounds of commitment that sexual intercourse forms the crescendo in a couple's marriage symphony.[1] We can attend a concert without the conductor, but the music will eventually prove sour to the ears until our only option seems to be to leave the auditorium. Sexual intercourse must be built on a foundation of personal and mutual commitment; without commitment, expressed through daily care and affirmation, intercourse is only a temporary satisfaction that will inevitably become a mere duty until the act itself seems intolerable.[2]

The hub around which the cycle of romance revolves is the strategy statements that commit each partner in the marriage to principles that protect the marriage from selfish ambition (see James 3:14–18). *Only selfishness can slow or stop the cycle of romance from turning and growing.* As the principles are being practiced, the natural tendency each partner has to pursue the relationship for personal pleasure and gain is controlled, and the tension that gives friction to the cycle lessens. Personal and mutual commitment is desired more because of the rewards that are won: physical, emotional, mental, and spiritual satisfaction. A romance should tell the story of a couple who committed themselves to the welfare of each other in a climate that begs for individuality. It should tell about a couple who played, cried, dreamed, and grieved together, whose romance ended not in the presence of a judge with harsh words and cutting glares, but at a grave side where one spouse thankfully remembered the love and sacrifice that exemplified a long and fruitful journey through the marriage marathon.

According to Minirth, Newman, and Hemfelt, a marriage must go through five passages if it is to last. They indirectly comment on the role that the cycle of romance plays within each of these passages:

> Each of the passages through which every married couple travels, like bases on a softball diamond, must be appropriately dealt with if the next one is to count. And the *tasks that accompany these passages must be completed* before the next task commences. By tasks we mean attitude changes one must make and jobs one must complete in order to maintain an intimate marital relationship [emphasis added].[3]

The tasks and attitudes to which these writers allude are the commitments (strategy statements) and principles that allow the cycle of romance to revolve as a couple progresses in the marriage marathon. If the tires on a bicycle lose air pressure, the riders are not able to focus on the commitments that are necessary for winning the marathon. Flat tires do the cyclists no good! So also, a satisfying cycle of romance is dependent on the previous commitments (strategies) explained in this book. If, however, romance "loses its pressure" (is not nurtured), the participants in the marriage marathon find it more difficult to practice the commitments on which romance depends. Romance is both the product (reward) of the strategies and the impetus to keep these strategies alive.

The Five Languages of Romance

How do *you* say "I love you"? What about your spouse? What says "I love you" to one person may not mean the same thing to another. Cal regularly hugged Nicole. Every morning he would kiss her goodbye as they each departed for work. You can imagine his surprise when Nicole told him that she wasn't sure that he loved her anymore. It wasn't that she didn't want him to kiss and hug her or that she didn't appreciate it. Nicole reminded Cal that when they dated he was always so thoughtful when he remembered to bring her a small token of his love when he came home from a trip or when he was going to take her out on a date. Over the last few months Cal had unconsciously let that habit go by the wayside, sending a message to Nicole that he might be tiring of her. Nothing could have been further from the truth. To Cal, Nicole's love for him was expressed by physical touch; a back rub was a clear indication to him that she adored him. The mistake Cal made was to assume that his language of romance was the same as Nicole's. To Nicole, romance was kept lively and stable by occasional gifts. Nicole was a little surprised to find out that the gifts she had been giving Cal had little significance compared to that lingering good-bye kiss at the door.

Gary Chapman has suggested that there are five primary languages through which people give and receive love.[4] These languages are stimulants for romance; they become the acts of honor and encouragement that meet our spouses' need for security in the relationship and pave the path to satisfying sexual intimacy. Individuals may interact in each of these five areas, but many people seem to respond to one language more than the others. Carole Mayhall reminds us that

> when we have learned our partner's language of love, then we can begin to build the secondary languages into our relationship—and have lots of creative, wonderful times doing it. But if we are missing the primary language, our partner may not feel loved in any other way and our efforts will go unnoticed.[5]

Words of affirmation may mean more to one spouse than another. Telling your spouse that you appreciate his or her efforts with the kids or reminding your spouse that his or her financial skills give you peace of mind can be one of the most loving things you do in an entire day. Each time a word of encouragement or appreciation is given, it affirms your commitment and love to your spouse. Your spouse feels loved when honor and respect is given verbally and without prompting.

Those of you whose primary stimulus for romance comes from your partner's commitment to *quality time* together will feel loved and appreciated when time is intentionally dedicated to your welfare and that of the marriage. A date to a private location gives those of you with this love language comfort and stability in the union. A picnic alone on the beach, a discussion in a place without distractions, meals together, or a vacation that centers around or creates couple interaction are all great relationship boosters. Those of you who speak the language of quality time feel loved when your spouse values face-to-face time with you.

While some of you may be made more comfortable because your partner dedicates time to the relationship, others may consider the *giving or receiving of a gift* to be the ultimate "I love you" statement. There seems to be a special symbolism behind gift-giving; it is not always the gift that matters (the cost and size are not often important), but the thought and the time taken to go out and shop for it. Gifts can also take the form of an unexpected night out for dinner and a movie, a cool drink given on a hot afternoon, or a quiet period created so that you can rest. These gifts say, "I love you!" It is important that those of you whose primary love language is something *other than gifts* be sensitive to the statement behind the gift that is given by one whose primary love language *is gifts*. It is easier to show love in one's own language than in the language of another; in marriage, you must learn to speak fluently in at least one other language—the language of your spouse. Those of you who speak the language of giving or receiving gifts feel loved by spontaneous offerings and gifts from your spouse.

A fourth language understands love through *acts of service*. Those of you who speak this language love to serve and feel loved when your spouse does special things for you. You like to have things done for you without having to ask. If you must always ask your spouse for help, you don't view your spouse's act of service as a response of the heart. Rather it is an obligation met. Those of you who give and receive love in this language are excellent workers who naturally do a lot for your family. You can be easily hurt, however, by a partner who sits back and enjoys the fruit of your efforts without ever responding in kind. Those of you who naturally serve to express your love need to be served if romance is to continue spiraling in a positive direction. You feel loved when your partner does things that you would like done.

Finally, some of you believe that love is expressed through the *physical touch* of your spouse. A hug, kiss, back rub, and the sensual side of love creates relational stability in the hearts of those of you who operate from this language. You are society's huggers. Touch is the critical ingredient in developing a loving relationship; without it, you can feel abandoned and lost in the relationship. When your spouse simply places a hand on your shoulder during a movie, it speaks volumes to those of you whose love language is touch-centered. Sexual intercourse is very important to you, and caution needs to be taken not to underestimate the rejection you feel when sex is often denied or believed unimportant by a spouse with a different love language. You feel loved when physical touch is voluntarily given by your partner.

When we commit to meeting the needs of our spouses 100 percent of the time, we must not forget to always include romantic needs. The cycle of romance has its impetus in this initial strategy. To keep the adventure going, you must learn the romantic language of your partner or suffer the consequences of living out a novel with no comedy or climax.

The Transition Statement

Romance develops in a relationship that is nurtured with daily care and is based on principles void of selfish ambition. The growth that you desire is inseparably linked to your willingness to change selfish attitudes that put off romance. Change isn't easy, but when good can come from it, there is no other alternative. Completing the marriage marathon is not a given; it is hard, selfless work that comes through daily acts of the will. These strategies and principles have been provided so that you will have the tools for putting together a successful marriage marathon. Now you must ask yourself if you have the courage to accept these strategies and the stamina to consistently apply them.

"I will place my spouse's needs before my own."

"I will daily love, honor, and encourage my spouse."

"I will practice a style of communication that allows my spouse to be vulnerable and honest at all times."

"I will seek resolution and growth during conflict."

"I will set timely and realistic goals with my spouse."

"I will nurture romance through daily care."

You have just passed Marriage Marathon Milestone 6. Congratulations!

Conclusion

*W*hat keeps us focused on an unconditional type of love that is not natural to any human being? What motivation exists to encourage us to fight our natural inclination to love for our own bene-fit? The answers to these questions are found in the fact that someone has loved us in the way we are to love our spouses. He has also provided us with an example of how we are to live. We who have experienced the love of Christ are compelled to love in a similar manner. His caring and unconditional love is profoundly set forth for all humanity in the story of a woman who is shunned by society but is destined to meet a Person, at an isolated well in a foreign country, who longs to change her life and help her meet her potential.

The actual ability to maintain the commitments proposed in this book are found in a faith that is eternally bound to the Person who is the originator of the institution of marriage. The selfish side of each of us can only be controlled by a daily desire to lose ourselves to the purpose and plan of a sovereign God.

In Search of the Heart

We'd like to share three stories with you. Our entire focus throughout this book has been on relationships in general and on your relationship with your spouse in specific. You've read this book because that relationship is important to you, and you want to sustain and improve it. Yet sometimes, as individuals, we are not very good at relationships. For whatever reason, be it fear or frustration, lack of experience, lack of skill, or past failure, we don't seem to do as well at relationships as we wish we would. We want the right thing, but we just don't know how to make it happen or how to find it. Perhaps we are, as expressed in the lyrics of a song, "Looking for love in all the wrong places, looking for love in too many faces." Have you felt like that? The gospel of John tells the story of just such a person. Read John's story and see how Jesus touched the life of a woman who had looked for love in all the wrong faces and places.

The Search for a Woman's Heart

Now he had to go through Samaria. So he came to a town in Samaria called Sychar, near the plot of ground Jacob had given to his son Joseph. Jacob's well was there, and Jesus, tired as he was from the journey, sat down by the well. It was about the sixth hour.

When a Samaritan woman came to draw water, Jesus said to her, "Will you give me a drink?" (His disciples had gone into town to buy food.)

The Samaritan woman said to him, "You are a Jew and I am a Samaritan woman. How can you ask me for a drink?" (For Jews do not associate with Samaritans.)

Jesus answered her, "If you knew the gift of God and who it is that asks you for a drink, you would have asked him and he would have given you living water."

"Sir," the woman said, "you have nothing to draw with and the well is deep. Where can you get this living water? Are you greater than our father Jacob, who gave us the well and drank from it himself, as did also his sons and his flocks and herds?"

Jesus answered, "Everyone who drinks from this water will be thirsty again, but whoever drinks the water I give him will never thirst. Indeed, the water I give him will become a spring of water welling up to eternal life."

The woman said to him, "Sir, give me this water so that I won't get thirsty and have to keep coming here to draw water."

He told her, "Go, call your husband and come back."

"I have no husband," she replied.

Jesus said to her, "You are right when you say you have no husband. The fact is, you have had five husbands, and the man you now have is not your husband. What you have just said is quite true."

"Sir," the woman said, "I can see that you are a prophet. Our fathers worshiped on this mountain, but you Jews claim that the place where we must worship is in Jerusalem."

Jesus declared, "Believe me, woman, a time is coming when you will worship the Father neither on this mountain nor in Jerusalem. You Samaritans worship what you do not know; we worship what we do know, for salvation is from the Jews. Yet a time is coming and has now come when the true worshipers will worship the Father in spirit and truth, for they are the kind of worshipers the Father seeks. God is spirit, and his worshipers must worship in spirit and truth."

The woman said, "I know that Messiah" (called Christ) "is coming. When he comes, he will explain everything to us."

Then Jesus declared, "I who speak to you am he."

Just then the disciples returned and were surprised to find him talking with a woman. But no one asked, "What do you want?" or "Why are you talking with her?"

Then, leaving her water jar, the woman went back to the town and said to the people, "Come, see a man who told me everything I ever did. Could this be the Christ?" They came out of town and made their way to him. . . .

Many of the Samaritans from that town believed in him because of the woman's testimony, "He told me everything I ever did.". . . And because of his words, many more became believers. (John 4:4–30, 39, 41)

Let's consider the woman at the well. Perhaps as we look at her story we will see a little of our own story or the story of someone we love. She was certainly concerned about relationships. Can you picture her story in your mind? What are the dynamics of her story? Surely it is one of sorrow and sadness, disappointment and despair.

The choices she has made in life and in love have brought neither lasting romance nor respect. She comes to this well with an empty water container *and* an empty heart. Just as she has returned repeatedly to the well for physical sustenance, so also has she drawn repeatedly from the well of romance, searching for emotional sustenance. Now everything is empty again. On this day as she treks to the well, she has few joys and many regrets. Of her mood and misery, one writer noted:

The torrents of passion, once swift in her life, have now run their course. She is weathered and worn, her face eroded by the gullies of a spent life. . . . Accusing thoughts are her only companions as she ponders the futile road her life has traveled. She thinks back to the crossroads in her life, of roads that might have been taken, of happiness that might have been shared, of dreams that might have been fulfilled. But she knows that she can never go back. . . . For her, marriage has been a retreating mirage. Again and again she has returned to the matrimonial well, hoping to draw from it something to quench her thirst for love and happiness. But again and again she has left that well disappointed. And so, under the weight of such thoughts she comes to Jacob's well, her empty water jar a telling symbol of her life.[1]

Have you stood in her shoes at the same well or a similar one? Was it in the distant past or recent past? Perhaps it is even today.

But what happens to her? She meets one who addresses her without condemnation or scorn. He speaks of her past and present marital status, but He does not belittle or castigate her. The Lord never scrapes our wounds; He only soothes them. He does not desire to handle us harshly; He longs to hold us tenderly. With a love and gentleness that she has always desired but never received, He tells this unnamed Samaritan woman that the most important relationship she can ever have is with God, not with a man. That relationship comes through Jesus Christ alone. Only when she understands and accepts this relationship will other relationships begin to be what God has intended. Looking for love in all the wrong places, looking for love in too many faces—until she came face-to-face with the one who is Himself the embodiment and fullness of love.

What we learn from the woman at the well is that if we want to have success in our relationships, especially in our marriages, then we must first have a proper relationship with God. Our interpersonal or horizontal relationships will never fully succeed until our spiritual or vertical relationship is right. You can't get things right permanently with your spouse or the world until you get things right with God. *Ultimately, the quality of your relationship with God will determine the quality of your relationship with your spouse.*

In the same way that you desire a living and vibrant relationship with your spouse, so does God desire a living and vibrant relationship with you. The Bible says that God desires to have a relationship with each of you, but that possibility has been temporarily broken and marred by sin and its many selfish faces. Please remember that God will not force Himself on you. Start your search for Him from where you are today; you won't miss Him. He is only a prayer away.

God is searching for hurting hearts. It is not His desire to see us fail, but we do fail and live with wounded hearts, not because of God, but because we believe that we can live outside His design for our lives.

The Search for a Man's Heart

There is a second story about a man whose life paralleled and perhaps exceeded the suffering, insecurity, and pain of the woman at the well. He lived three hundred fifty years later, in North Africa. He had many relationships, one of which produced a son he dearly loved with a woman who was not his wife and whom he did not love. Unable to find peace in relationships and the pleasures of his society—which include wine, women, and song—he fled North Africa and sailed to Italy where he turned to philosophy and education. In the midst of this, he converted to Christianity.

He returned to North Africa to share his newfound faith. It is said that when he arrived at his homeland and left the ship, he passed on the pier a former lover who called out to him, "Augustine, Augustine, it is I!" In a telling moment he continued on his way and, turning, said to her, "Yes, but it is not I."

He later wrote a famous autobiography entitled *Confessions,* in which he wrote regarding our relationship with God, "Our heart knows no rest until it finds its rest in Thee!" It was true of the woman at the well, it was true of Augustine, and it is true of us. The search for significance and success will succeed only if it begins with God. True happiness comes not from following the ways of the world, but the ways of the Lord. It's true in our quest for immortality, and it's true in our quest for meaningful marriages.

The Search for Your Heart

We come now to the third and final story, that of someone living today. It is your story. We know the story of the woman at the well and we know the story of Augustine, but we do not know your story. But you know your story, and God knows your story. You can keep no secrets from God. He knows your past as well as your present and your future. And He stands by, waiting for you at the well of personal reflection, hoping that you will look in His direction for the answers that resolve eternal questions, repair wounded hearts, and reunite faltering relationships.

Ultimately we are all the same—we are all broken, and we are searching for love and significance. The Bible says that regardless of who we are or what we have done, God loves us. He loves us so much that He sent Jesus Christ, His Son, to die on a cross for our sins. Because of this, if we ask for and accept His offer of salvation, we can have not only fullness of life in the present, but the assurance of life in eternity.

We are all searching, but so is God. He is looking for us. The Bible says that while we were yet sinners, Christ died for us. God is searching for us and is willing to reach down into our turmoil and troubles to give us true significance. Look for love in the right place; look for love on the right Face, and you will find the motivation and reason to live out the strategies of marriage presented in this book. Success in marriage is not so much a matter of finding the right person but of being the right person. You can and may find the right person without God, but you will never be the right person without God. Grow in your relationship with God and you will grow in your relationship with your spouse.

The selfless and unconditional love God imparted to us on the cross is the foundation for the selfless and unconditional love that you impart to your spouse. Make the most of your journey together by choosing to know and obey the Lord of life, the One whose love we seek to reflect in this life through the institution of marriage. In the marriage marathon, never forget that ultimate victory comes not on earth, but in heaven when you can stand before God and hear your Savior say that your marriage has been a reflection of His love for the church and for the world. Take care of your relationship with your spouse and you will become a beautiful and vibrant illustration of all that we have talked about in these pages. But more importantly, take care of your heart and soul, which you will have for all eternity.

Making the Most of Your Wedding

*T*he information in this appendix is provided in the form of suggestions that we believe will bring extra meaning to your upcoming wedding or the wedding of someone you know. A wedding ceremony is more than a thirty-minute pageant that precedes an expensive party, and it is more than a procedure to be followed, as if completing it gives the marriage a better chance of success. A wedding ceremony is many things to many people. It is the public showing of a couple's love and devotion to God and to one another. It is the joining of two people in an inseparable union—a promise to God that they will not allow their union to be dissolved or violated by anything short of death. It is the joining of two families who provide history as well as security and identity to the couple's offspring. For the parents, it is both a blessing and a loss—though each of the parents gains a child, they also must deal with the reality that they are also saying good-bye to a child. For friends, the wedding ceremony may bring substantial change to a childhood or teen friendship because the friend they love must now devote less energy to friendships and more to his or her marriage. The wedding ceremony is a moment that showplaces the numerous commitments that the couple, their parents, siblings, immediate and extended family, friends, and witnesses must make to support a new and sacred marriage union. It is a time of purity and honesty that must shape the future if needs are to be identified and met, if honor and encouragement are going to flow from a love that is unconditional, if communication is going to produce personal and mutual growth, if conflicts are to be resolved, and if romance is to be nurtured.

For these reasons and many more, it is important that creative ideas be considered that help everyone who attends a wedding understand more fully what wedding-ceremony traditions are all about. The two suggestions that follow help bring greater meaning to what parents do when they give their daughter to another, and help to provide greater understanding of what the marrying couple is vowing to each other. Don't be afraid to create a new tradition if doing so gives a clearer and more meaningful understanding of God's original design for the marriage union.

Suggestion I

The giving of a daughter by a father (or by the mother and father) happens so quickly at the beginning of a wedding ceremony that its significance is mostly lost, forgotten, or at best regarded as a tradition for which few give a second thought. As a father, I (Gary) found this to be a moment of great significance. I wanted my future son-in-law to never forget what I was doing, how I felt about it, or what I expected of him. For this reason I wrote the statement that begins at the bottom of this page. The pastor asked, "Who gives this woman to this man?" Before I answered "Her mother and I," I reached into my pocket and pulled out a piece of paper, and then proceeded to read. Though it was difficult to get through, I consider it one of the most important statements I have ever made. I know that other fathers have wanted to do something similar, but tradition is often hard to alter. Please feel free to use this statement in any way that helps you to make the most of your wedding or that of your child.

The Giving of a Daughter

This is one of those special days that you think about from the day God blesses you with the birth of a child. It is also a day that brings some measure of sadness. In a few moments I will relinquish many, if not most, of the responsibilities that I have for Lindsay as a parent and especially as a father. Though I have not done all that I wish I had done for Lindsay in preparing her for this day, I know that I have done what I could. Though raising her has not always been easy, I have always loved her and always will. Today, the major provider of her love and care moves from Kathie and I and falls on the shoulders and heart of Jeff Brown. For this reason, my request to Jeff is that he never forsake the faith that

God has so graciously given to him, and that he continues to grow in that faith in order to be the husband that both God and I, as Lindsay's father, expect him to be. It is both Jeff's and Lindsay's faith in Christ that will give them the strength to weather the inevitable challenges that await them. As you both persistently seek the Lord, you will always know His intimate presence and ultimately discover His impeccable purposes. Jeff, I want you to know that Kathie and I welcome you into our family and that we receive you without reservation or regret. Love, honor, and encourage our daughter as we expect her to love, honor, and encourage you. What you do now is for life—honor God, your family, and mine by never forsaking the vows you make this day. I want but two sons in my life. You are the first of two. Lord willing, my daughter, Katie, will provide me with the second.

Suggestion 2

When I started doing weddings, I wanted to add something just prior to the vows that was very personal and thoughtful. I decided to ask the groom and the bride each to prepare a letter that would express his or her personal understanding of the relationship each had with the other, of the commitment each would soon make to the other, and of the reason each felt compelled to marry this one person to whom he or she would devote the rest of his or her life. Though many thought it would be quite challenging to write, most couples finished the task and were glad they did. The following are the letters that my dear friends Paul and Andrea Czerniak prepared. Just before they shared their vows of love and commitment, I asked Paul and Andrea to face one another and hold each other's hands. Then I read the letters to them and to the witnesses of the wedding (though I always offer to let the couple read their own letters to one another, only one couple has decided to do so, as yet). This addition has always helped to make the wedding ceremony more meaningful and memorable for the couple as well as for the family and witnesses.

Paul's Letter to Andrea

Andrea,

How can I begin to explain the love that I have for you? As I look to the day that we will be married, I get a feeling of excitement, as well as a feeling of responsibility. My excitement ranges from the physical to the spiritual. You are truly beautiful, and with that beauty, God has given you a tender, compassionate heart. You have been willing to serve Him, and desire a relationship centered around Him. Here lies my responsibility in leading us according to His Word. What a challenge!

Looking back, it's ironic that we didn't date each other in college, even though we each thought about it. Instead we were just friends. I have always wanted to marry someone who was my best friend, and now God has granted my desire. I enjoy everything about you, and I enjoy spending every minute with you. From the baseball games to the quiet times we share, you are an inspiration to me.

I can tell that you love me with all your heart, and I love you with all my heart, too. I want to be everything for you. I want to provide for you, and be there for you to lean on. I want you to share with me your deepest desires, cares, and dreams. I want to be a team because together in Christ we can conquer whatever challenge we may face. God has entrusted your care with me, and I plan to give you my all!

I heard a saying several weeks ago that sums up what I am trying to convey. It has been said that "You don't marry the woman that you can live with; you marry the woman that you can't live without." I can't live without you, and I thank God that I won't have to. I love you!

Paul

Andrea's Letter to Paul

Paul,

How can I tell you how much I love you on a sheet of paper? On a sheet of paper you cannot see the smile that lights my face every time I see you. You cannot see my eyes that say, "I love you through and through." You cannot feel my hugs that squeeze so tight, saying "I never want to let you go," nor can you hear my voice that whispers "*te amo*" every time you are near. You know that I love you with all my heart and soul, but there is so much more.

Paul, throughout my whole life the Lord has guided and protected me, and He has placed men in my life to do the same. He has given me my dad, who married a faithful Christian woman, coached my softball teams, sat out on the porch waiting for me when I was late for my curfew, and hugs me when I do well and when I'm down. He gave me my "adopted brother," Gary, who threatened to "hurt" any guy who would hurt me, didn't want me to date until I was thirty, let me drive his car to Chicago only days after getting my driver's permit, and encourages me through tears and smiles just as a big brother should. Now, Paul, it's your turn. God has been preparing you throughout your whole life to be the number-one man in my life who will love, protect, encourage, and support me throughout our lifetime together. You are an answer to many prayers and more wonderful than I could ever dream or desire. Today I am committing myself to spending the rest of my life with you, and I am so excited.

I commit to you all that I am, all that I have, and all that I will become. You have swept me off my feet and you make me feel like the most important person in the world. Your love has helped heal hurts, and your hugs and patience have allowed me to open up a part of me that no one has seen before. Because of your commitment to Christ, I can place my complete trust in you and I want to share with you my innermost thoughts and dreams. You do so much for me, even the little things; I can't help but want to be the very best for you. You are already the best for me, and I could go on and on about everything I love about you. You love God and want us to serve Him, and you are a great leader for us and will be for our family. I will follow you wherever you go and I will always be by your side. You make me so happy, and I am a better person because you are in my life. We have so much fun together; you have become my best friend. I look forward to sharing each and every moment that the days and years ahead will bring.

Paul, you are my inspiration and sunshine. I cannot express how grateful to God I am for you. Whether we are up or down, I promise to give 100 percent to us. I promise to grow and mature with you. I am so proud that in a few moments you will be my husband. We are a great team. Through our obedience to the Lord and our love for Him, we will be together for life. I love you.

Andrea

Endnotes

Introduction

1. Ross Campbell, *How to Really Love Your Teenager* (Wheaton, Ill.: Victor, 1993), 24.
2. Kevin Costner, *People Magazine* 42 (7 November 1994).
3. Hans Walter Wolff, *Anthropology of the Old Testament* (Philadelphia: Fortress, 1974), 40. See also pages 40–58 for a discussion of the semantic range of this term in relation to the human condition.
4. Colin Brown, ed., *The New International Dictionary of New Testament Theology,* vol. 2 (Grand Rapids: Zondervan, 1976), 180–84. Gerhard Kittel, ed., *Theological Dictionary of the New Testament,* vol. 3 (Grand Rapids: Eerdmans, 1965), 605–14.
5. David Allen, *In Search of the Heart* (Nashville: Nelson, 1993), 8.
6. A full discussion on the definition of love will be presented later in this volume.

Chapter 1: Failing to Reach the Finish Line

1. Costner, *People* 42 (7 November 1994).
2. *Time* (27 February 1995), 49.

Chapter 2: A Bicycle Built for Two

1. Larry Crabb, *The Marriage Builder* (Grand Rapids: Zondervan, 1992), 27–30. Larry Crabb describes the need for purpose and value as significance and the need to love and be loved as security.
2. See H. Norman Wright, *Beating the Blues: Overcoming Depression and Stress* (Ventura, Calif.: Regal, 1988), 5–17.
3. Barbara Kantrowitz with Pat Wingert, "Breaking the Divorce Cycle" in *Newsweek* (13 January 1992), 48–53.
4. Sharon M. Sneed and Joe S. McIlhaney, *PMS: What It Is and What You Can Do About It* (Grand Rapids: Baker, 1988), 8. This book is an excellent resource for every husband so that he can understand the symptoms and extremities faced by the woman he loves who must endure PMS.

Chapter 3: Know Who Else Is Peddling!

1. For a complete study of the differences between men and women, see John Gray, *Men, Women, and Relationships* (Hillsboro, Ore.: Beyond Words, 1993), 37–105. Gary Smalley, *The Joy of Committed Love* (Grand Rapids: Zondervan, 1984), 9–20. Zondervan now publishes Smalley's book under the title *Hidden Keys of a Loving Lasting Relationship*. See also Jack and Carole Mayhall, *Opposites Attack: Turning Differences into Opportunities* (Colorado Springs: NavPress, 1990), 29–57.

2. Anne Moir and David Jessel, *Brain Sex: The Real Difference Between Men and Women* (New York: Dell, 1989), 5, 8.

3. See Chris Evatt, *He and She: A Lively Guide to Understanding the Opposite Sex* (New York: MJF Books, 1992).

4. For a complete look at the biological differences between men and women, see Joe Tanenbaum, *Male and Female Realities* (Costa Mesa, Calif.: Tanenbaum Associates, 1990), 29–50.

5. Michael Segell, "The Unfeeling Brute" in *Esquire* 125, no. 3 (March 1996): 60. Studies show that these male and female emotional differences may be due to a larger presence of the chemical serotonin in the female system. See also Gray, *Men, Women, and Relationships,* 59: "Men see the world from a 'focused perspective' while women see the world from a more 'expanded perspective.' Both perceptions are equally accurate. Masculine awareness tends to relate one thing to another in a sequential way, gradually building a complete picture. It is a perspective that relates one part to another part, in terms of producing a whole. Feminine awareness is expanded: it intuitively takes in the whole picture and gradually discovers the parts within, and it explores how the parts are all related to the whole. It places more emphasis on context rather than content."

6. Cf. John Gray, *Men Are from Mars, Women Are from Venus* (New York: HarperCollins, 1992), 16–41, and Tanenbaum, *Male and Female Realities,* 133–38.

7. Evatt, *He and She,* 120–21.

8. "Conservative estimates from sex researchers note that when it comes to sexual readiness and arousal, a husband can become fully aroused in *ninety seconds,* whereas a wife can take between fifteen and *thirty minutes"* (John Trent, *Love for All Seasons: Eight Ways to Nurture Intimacy* [Chicago: Moody Press, 1996], 134).

9. "While men virtually jump-start into an active sexuality—hitting their peak in their late teens through early twenties—women generally take longer to feel at ease with their desires. A young woman new to sex often finds her enjoyment has less to do with physical pleasure than emotional needs that sex can fulfill: attention, acceptance, and feeling attractive. Negative societal or family messages about sex can dampen her enthusiasm, as can performance anxiety." Many women describe the thirties as their most fulfilling time sexually. See Judith D. Schwartz, "Your Sexual Stages" in *Redbook* 182, no. 3 (January 1994):53.

10. Smalley, *The Joy of Committed Love.*

Chapter 4: Winning the Race Together

1. See "Boy Scouts and Girl Scouts" in Gray, *Men, Women and Relationships,* 60–61.

2. Evatt, *He and She,* 150–51. See also Willard F. Harley Jr., *His Needs, Her Needs* (Grand Rapids: Revell, 1986), 27–39.

3. Evatt, *He and She,* 150.

Chapter 5: The Many Faces of Love

1. Brown, *Dictionary of N.T. Theology,* 2:539.

2. The words *storgē* and *epithymia* are used in this way by H. Norman Wright in a video entitled, *Marriage: For Lovers Only,* vol. 2, *How to Add Sizzle to Your Marriage* (Dallas, Tex.: Priority One Publishers).

3. Brown, *Dictionary of N.T. Theology,* 2:539.

4. Ibid.

5. Stated by an interviewee in the video series *Marriage: For Lovers Only,* vol. 2, *How to Add Sizzle to Your Marriage.*

6. W. E. Vine, *An Expository Dictionary of New Testament Words with Their Precise Meanings for English Readers,* 17th impression (Old Tappan, N.J.: Revell, 1966), 21.

Chapter 6: Making Marriage's Honor Roll

1. *Kābôd* is also translated "glory" in reference to Yahweh. He is glorious and worthy of honor not only because of the position He holds, but also because of the unmatched character with which He reigns (Ps. 24:7–10).
2. R. Laird Harris, Gleason L. Archer Jr., and Bruce K. Waltke, eds., *Theological Wordbook of the Old Testament,* vol. 2 (Chicago: Moody Press, 1980), 426–27.
3. Brown, *Dictionary of N.T. Theology,* 2:48–51.

Chapter 7: Encouragement: Turning Possibility into Progress

1. Brown, *Dictionary of N.T. Theology,* 3: 349–50. *Artios,* and its derivatives, *katartizø, katartisis* (2 Cor. 13:9), and *katartismos* (Eph. 4:12) look at improving an individual to the point of complete usefulness. See 2 Tim. 3:17, "All Scripture is inspired by God and profitable for teaching . . . that the man of God may be adequate, *equipped* for every good work" (NASB). It is interesting to note that *katartismon* in Ephesians 4:12, "the equipping of the saints," is "a medical term referring to the setting of a fracture." See *Dictionary of N.T. Theology,* 1:302.

Chapter 8: Creating a Lasting Legacy

1. Carl F. H. Henry, *Carl Henry at His Best: A Lifetime of Quotable Thoughts* (Portland, Ore.: Multnomah, 1989), 143.
2. Shervert H. Frazier, "Psychotrends: Taking Stock of Tomorrow's Family and Sexuality" in *Psychology Today* 27, no. 1 (January–February 1994): 32. This article is worth the reading for those interested in understanding the depths to which the sexual revolution has yet to take us. However, the article favors the decline of the traditional family for free sexual expression.
3. Council on Families in America, *Marriage in America: A Report to the Nation* (March 1995), 3. See also Maggie Gallagher, *The Abolition of Marriage: How We Destroy Lasting Love* (Washington, D.C.: Regnery, 1996).
4. Council on Families in America, *Marriage in America: A Report to the Nation* (March 1995), 3. See also David Van Biema, "The Price of a Broken Home" in *Time* (27 February 1995), 53.
5. Francis A. Schaeffer, *How Should We Then Live? The Rise and Decline of Western Thought and Culture* (Old Tappan, N.J.: Revell, 1976), 205.
6. Council on Families in America, *Marriage in America: A Report to the Nation* (March 1995), 4.
7. The consequences of divorce are traumatic. "Compared with people who have grown up in intact families, adult children of divorce are more likely to have troubled relationships and broken marriages. A desire for stability sends some down the aisle at too young an age, and they wind up in divorce court not long afterward. Others fear commitment because they learned too well the lessons of their childhood—don't trust anyone, not even Mom or Dad. Even when divorce releases children from their parents' violent or emotionally abusive marriage, they worry that they don't know how to be half of a happy couple *because they've never seen one close up at home*" (emphasis added) (Barbara Kantrowitz and Pat Wingert, "Breaking the Divorce Cycle" in *Newsweek* [13 January 1992]: 49).
8. Frazier, "Psychotrends," 32.

Strategy 3: Effective Communication:
Evaluating the Health of Your Marriage

1. Sherod Miller's research over the past twenty-eight years explains why counselors often hear their clients complain about their lack of communication. "Communication, both nonverbal and verbal, is the 'stuff' that *initiates, builds, maintains, and destroys relationships*. It is simultaneously a *vehicle* for relating and an *index* of the relationship" (emphases added). Couples who don't relate well aren't communicating well (Sherod Miller, Daniel Wackman, Elam Nunnally, and Phyllis Miller, *Connecting with Self and Others* [Littleton, Colo.: Interpersonal Communication Programs, 1988], 9). H. Norman Wright provides insight into the reason why the lack of communication is detrimental to marriage. "Marriage is an intimate relationship built on mutual understanding, but in order to truly understand another person you must be able to communicate with him. A husband and wife can know a great deal *about* each other without really knowing one another. Communication is the process that allows people to know each other, to relate to one another, to understand the true meaning of the other person's life" (H. Norman Wright, *Communication: Key to Your Marriage* [Ventura, Calif.: Regal, 1974], 63).

Chapter 9: Setting a Foundation with Honesty and Vulnerability

1. Miller, Wackman, Nunally, and Miller, *Connecting with Self and Others,* 45–78. Compare Sherod Miller's description of four styles of communication (Shop Talk, Control Talk, Search Talk, and Straight Talk) in which each of us communicate. These four styles delineate certain levels of communication. For a list of these five levels of communication mentioned in reverse order, see Wright, *Communication: Key to Your Marriage,* 67–69.

2. Cf. Wright, *Communication: Key to your Marriage,* 160–63.

Chapter 11: Developing Better Communication Skills

1. The following "Explaining Skills" and "Understanding Skills" have been adapted from a couples communication course produced by Interpersonal Communications Programs, Inc., Littleton, Colorado.

Chapter 12: Understanding the Power of Forgiveness

1. For an excellent treatment on the subject of forgiveness, see Charles Stanley, *Victory Over Life's Challenges: The Gift of Forgiveness* (New York: Inspirational Press, 1995), 365–547.

2. Forgiveness is primarily a religious phenomenon that has recently provoked great interest in the scientific community. Though some studies have been done and show results, the empirical minds of the modernists remain suspicious, but keenly interested. See Michael E. McCullough and Everett L. Worthington Jr., "Encouraging Clients to Forgive People Who Have Hurt Them: Review, Critique, and Research Perspective," *Journal of Psychology and Theology* 22, no. 1 (1994): 3–20.

Chapter 13: Bringing Style into the Journey

1. Albert Metowbian, *Silent Messages* (Belmont, Calif.: Wadsworth, 1971), 42–44. Seven percent is content, 38 percent is tone, and 55 percent is nonverbal.

2. Gary Smalley and John Trent, *The Two Sides of Love* (Colorado Springs: Focus on the Family, 1990).

3. H. Norman Wright, *Holding on to Romance* (Ventura, Calif.: Regal, 1992), 151–55, provides a test and instruction on the value of knowing your spouse's sensory

style of communication (visual, auditory, or feeling). This insight into communication can be helpful if your spouse happens to lean heavily toward one area over another.

4. Gary Smalley and John Trent, *The Language of Love* (Colorado Springs: Focus on the Family, 1988), 34. The resource they quote is: J. Levy, "The Adaptive Advantages of Cerebral Asymmetry and Communication," *Annals of the New York Academy of Sciences* 229:264–72.

5. Robert Kohn, "Patterns of Hemispheric Specialization in Pre-Schoolers," *Neuropsychologia* 12:505–12, and E. Zaidel, "Auditory Language Comprehension in the Right Hemisphere: A Comparison with Child Language," *Language Acquisition and Language Breakdown* (Baltimore: Johns Hopkins University Press, 1978).

6. See Deborah Tannen, *You Just Don't Understand* (New York: Random House, 1990).

7. Ibid.

8. Clarence L. Barnhart and Robert K. Barnhart, eds., *The New World Book Dictionary*, vols. L–Z (Chicago: World Book, 1989), 1827.

9. When tradition is kept for the sake of tradition, i.e., the meaning of the event is lost or no longer promotes a positive result, it becomes a rut that eventually leaves a vital relationship vexed without variety. Even a "time-honored tradition" can be changed or at least adjusted to maintain its value.

Chapter 14: Peddling Softly Through the Minefields

1. See Willard F. Harley Jr., *Love Busters: Overcoming the Habits That Destroy Romantic Love* (Grand Rapids: Baker, 1992), 26–101, for a discussion of five harmful traits that must be resolved.

2. Paul D. Meier, Frank B. Minirth, Frank B. Wichern, and Donald E. Ratcliff, *Introduction to Psychology and Counseling: Christian Perspectives and Applications*, 2d ed. (Grand Rapids: Baker, 1991), 78.

3. Ibid., 217–18.

4. Ken R. Canfield, *The Seven Secrets of Effective Fathers: Becoming the Father You Want to Be* (Wheaton, Ill.: Tyndale House, 1992), 121–22.

5. Meier, Minirth, Wichern, and Ratcliff, *Introduction to Psychology and Counseling*, 74–75.

6. Francis Collins, M.D., from a paper, "The Human Genome Project," presented at The Christian Stake in Genetics Conference, 19 July 1996, Trinity International University.

7. Sherod Miller, Phyllis Miller, Elam W. Nunnally, and Daniel B. Wackman, *Talking and Listening Together: Couple Communication* (Littleton, Colo.: Interpersonal Communications, 1991), 15–39. See also, Miller, Wackman, Nunnally, and Miller, *Connecting with Self and Others*, 91–96.

8. Irene Goldenberg and Herbert Goldenberg, *Family Therapy: An Overview*, 2d ed. (Pacific Grove, Calif.: Brooks/Cole, 1985), 167–76.

9. Irving B. Weiner, *Principles of Psychotherapy* (New York: Wiley and Sons, 1975), 110.

Chapter 15: Scouting the Course Ahead

1. Brenda Hunter, *Home by Choice: Creating Emotional Security in Children* (Portland, Ore.: Multnomah, 1991).

2. See Tom Minnery, ed., *Pornography: A Human Tragedy* (Wheaton, Ill.: Christianity Today, 1986).

3. For a discussion about resolving various types of conflict, see Harley, *Love Busters*, 104–64.

4. Cf. Richard and Mary Strauss, "Working Through Marital Conflict," in *Growing a Healthy Home,* ed. Mike Yorkey (Brentwood, Tenn.: Wolgemuth and Hyatt, 1990), 21–27.

Strategy 5: Goal-Setting: Planning Timely and Realistic Goals Together

1. Wes Roberts and H. Norman Wright, *Before You Say I Do: A Marriage Preparation Manual for Couples* (Eugene, Ore.: Harvest House, 1978), 30.

Strategy 6: Romance: Adding Zing to the Journey

1. Barnhart and Barnhart, eds., *The World Book Dictionary,* 1808.
2. Compare a discussion on the modern view of romance by Wright, *Holding on to Romance,* 22–24.
3. Fulfilling our spouses' wants enhances romance and should be one of our strongest desires; however, wants can only be met as time and resources allow and only after needs are met.

Chapter 18: Romance Happens When...

1. Linda Dillow, "How to Really Love Your Man," in *The Making of a Marriage: Everything You Need to Know to Keep Your Relationship Alive and Healthy* (Nashville: Nelson, 1993), 195–99.

Chapter 19: Romance Is for Everyone!

1. Couples who engage in premarital intercourse place the physical expression of commitment before the mental and practical expressions of commitment, and turn romance into a sexually focused necessity that shapes and defines love rather than a cyclical adventure or process that places sex as the culmination of a multitude of romantic activities. Here lies the difference between unhealthy and healthy romance. Premarital sex places an emphasis on the sex act, which undermines the process that makes and keeps intercourse beautiful and sustainable. Abstaining until marriage forces the couple to develop intimacy through courtship, which allows the sex act to be seen as a reward for daily care.
2. "While all these small loving actions may seem to be unrelated to sexual intimacy, they're not. My friend Kevin Lehmen had it right with the title of his book, *Sex Begins in the Kitchen.* He didn't mean that you grab your spouse in the midst of doing the dishes, but that doing the dishes is the best way to have your spouse grab you in a more romantic time and place" (Trent, *Love for All Seasons,* 137).
3. Frank and Mary Alice Minirth, Brian and Deborah Newman, and Robert and Susan Hemfelt, *Passages of Marriage* (Nashville: Nelson, 1991), 9.
4. Gary Chapman, *The Five Love Languages: How to Express Heartfelt Commitment to Your Mate* (Chicago: Northfield, 1992), 39–118.
5. Mayhall, *Opposites Attack,* 95.

Conclusion

1. Ken Gire, *Intimate Moments with the Savior* (Grand Rapids: Zondervan, 1989), 24, 26.

Recommended Reading

Aldrich, Sandra P. *Men Read Newspapers, Not Minds and Other Things I Wish I'd Known When I First Got Married*. Wheaton, Ill.: Tyndale House, 1996.

Allen, David. *In Search of the Heart*. Nashville: Nelson, 1993.

Campbell, Ross. *How to Really Love Your Teenager*. Wheaton, Ill.: Victor, 1993.

Chapman, Gary. *The Five Languages of Love*. Chicago: Northfield, 1992.

Crabb, Lawrence J. *Men and Women: Enjoying the Difference*. Grand Rapids: Zondervan, 1991.

Evatt, Chris. *He and She: A Lively Guide to Understanding the Opposite Sex*. New York: MJF Books, 1992.

Gallagher, Maggie. *The Abolition of Marriage*. Washington, D.C.: Regnery, 1996.

Gire, Ken. *Intimate Moments with the Savior*. Grand Rapids: Zondervan, 1989.

Gray, John. *Men Are from Mars, Women Are from Venus*. New York: HarperCollins, 1992.

Harley, Willard F., Jr. *His Needs Her Needs: Building an Affair-proof Marriage*. Grand Rapids: Revell, 1986.

Jenkins, Jerry B. *Loving Your Marriage Enough to Protect It*. Brentwood, Tenn.: Wolgemuth and Hyatt, 1989.

Mason, Mike. *The Mystery of Marriage*. Sisters, Ore.: Multnomah, 1985.

Miller, Sherod, Phyllis Miller, Elam W. Nunnally, and Daniel B. Wackman. *Connecting with Self and Others*. Littleton, Colo.: Interpersonal Communication Programs, 1992.

Moir, Anne, and David Jessel. *Brain Sex: The Real Difference Between Men and Women*. New York: Dell, 1989.

Rainey, Dennis, and Barbara Rainey. *Building Your Mate's Self-Esteem*. Nashville: Nelson, 1993.

Smalley, Gary, and John Trent. *Home Remedies: Timeless Prescriptions for Today's Family.* Sisters, Ore.: Multnomah, 1991.

————. *The Two Sides of Love.* Colorado Springs: Focus on the Family, 1990.

Tannen, Deborah. *You Just Don't Understand.* New York: Random House, 1990.

Thomas Nelson Publishers. *The Making of a Marriage: Everything You Need to Know to Keep Your Relationship Alive and Healthy.* Nashville: Nelson, 1993.

Trent, John. *Love for All Seasons: Eight Ways to Nurture Intimacy.* Chicago: Moody Press, 1996.

Wright, H. Norman. *Holding on to Romance: Keeping Your Marriage Alive and Passionate after the Honeymoon Years Are Over.* Ventura, Calif.: Regal, 1987.

If you would like to host a *Winning the Marriage Marathon* seminar, please contact the publicity department of Kregel Publications at 1-800-733-2607.